POTTY TRAINING LIKE A PRO

A STEP-BY-STEP GUIDE TO POTTY TRAIN A TODDLER IN ONE WEEK FOR DADS

ALFIE THOMAS

Copyright © 2022 by Alfie Thomas. All rights reserved. Printed in the United States of America. No part of this book may be used or reproduced in any manner whatsoever without written permission except in the case of brief quotations.

Copyright © 2022 by Alfie Thomas

All rights reserved. No part of this publication may be reproduced, distributed or transmitted in any form or by any means, including photocopying, recording or any other electronic or mechanical methods, without the prior written permission of the publisher, except in the case of brief quotations embodied in critical reviews and certain other noncommercial uses permitted by copyright law.

Although the publisher and the author have made every effort to ensure that the information in this book was correct at press time and while this publication is designed to provide accurate information in regard to the subject matter overall, the publisher and author assume no responsibility for errors, inaccuracies, omissions or any other inconsistences herein and hereby disclaim any liability to any party for any loss, damage or disruption caused by errors or omission, whether such errors or omissions result from negligence, accident or any other cause.

This publication is meant as a source of valuable information for the reader, however, it is not meant as a substitute for direct expertise assistance. If such level of assistance is required, the services of a competent professional should be sought.

CONTENTS

What a Poop-Tastrophe!   9

1. GETTING STARTED   17
   Before You Begin   22
   My Experience   25
   Remember   26

2. PERFECT TIMING   29
   When should potty training start?   29
   Emotional Growth Needed for Toilet Training   35
   Psychological Readiness and Motor Skills Needed for Toilet Training   41
   Cognitive and Verbal Skills Needed for Toilet Training   44
   Remember   48

3. THE STAGES AND METHODS   51
   The Stages   51
   Potty Training: Which Method is best?   53
   The 3-day Method   54
   Child-Oriented Potty Training   63
   Parent-led Potty Training   67
   Infant Potty Training   67
   What You Can Do   74
   What Not to Do   76
   Hygiene   78
   Remember   78

4. DROPPING THE DIAPERS — 81
Keep it Going — 84
Consistency is Key — 87
Potty Training Rewards for our Little Ones — 89

5. NIGHT-TIME POTTY TRAINING — 91
Why Does Night-time Potty Training Take Longer? — 91
Is My Child Ready for Night-time Potty Training? — 92
Tips for Night-time Potty-Training Success — 92
When Should I Be Concerned? — 93
What can I do if my Child is Still Wetting the bed Overnight? — 94

6. POTTY TRAINING A CHILD WITH SPECIAL NEEDS — 97
Training Considerations — 98
Tips to Make Potty Training Easier — 100
Resistance — 101
Specific Considerations — 102

7. POTTY TRAINING MULTIPLES — 113
How is Potty Training Multiples Different? — 114
Common Questions — 114
Tips for Training Twins — 116

8. A POTTY-TRAINING CHEAT SHEET — 121
Potty Training Prep — 121
Seven Must-haves for Potty Training — 122
Boys Only — 125
Travel Gear — 127
Remember — 128

9. TROUBLESHOOTING 131
Why Won't my Child Poop in the Potty? 131
How do I Avoid Potty Power Struggles? 134
How do I get my Childcare Provider on Board? 136
Why is my Child Regressing? 140

Time For Action! 145
Bibliography 151

For Mercy, Ava, and Mia

"*Potty training is 98% asking a toddler if they have to go to the potty, them saying "no", and then them peeing everywhere 2 minutes later.*"

— KIDSAREDORKS

WHAT A POOP-TASTROPHE!

By the time Mia, my youngest daughter, was born, Mirabelle and I were having marriage problems, and we unanimously decided to get a divorce. It sounds simple, but it was not! It was anything but. It was difficult for the both of us and the girls as well.

However, Mia was just one year old when the divorce was finalized, and because Mirabelle and I decided the children needed a healthy environment, we opted for shared custody and split all our responsibilities. We had to put aside our differences for the sake of our angels. It was not easy on any of us.

As a single father, it was difficult to navigate the waters with three young daughters. I tried my best, and I still do—to this day. After all, life is about effort, not perfection.

When Mirabelle and I potty trained our first two daughters, Mercy and Ava, it was easier because it was the two of us; hence, there was more support and assistance. However, I oversaw training Mia all alone when she was with me. Boy was that daunting! While Mercy and Ava's potty-training successes were milestones, Mia's accomplishments felt like an even bigger achievement for me.

By the age of 2, Mia was able to keep her diaper dry for a long stretch. Moreover, she could pee and poop in the potty seat when I would place her there. She was on a good trajectory, but it is not as easy as it sounds. Mia did not have enough motivation to use the toilet because she knew she had the alternative of the diaper. She was way too engaged in her play time and did not like to take time out to use the bathroom. No thank you, sir!

I could see the signs, rocking back and forth, clenching her fist, and so on, and I knew she had to use to bathroom. However, she chose to use her diaper instead. There were so many moments where I would prod her and say, "Darling, let's go use the potty," and her response would be, "I fine, you go." This was frustrating to say the least. While rewards and praise did work on Mercy and Ava, they did not work too well with Mia.

So, I decided to change the reward system slightly. I bought her a swanky Barbie car and some big girl underwear to make the transition seem appealing and grown up. I showed her where I stored them and told her, "Mia darling, I will be placing these in the closet here. Whenever you begin to use the potty full-time, which I know you can, you can use these. Once you start wearing these, no more diapers for you honey, so tell me whenever you are ready!"

Boy oh boy, did that give her a kick start. She said goodbye to her diapers and was extremely excited about potty training from then on. I patted myself on the back for being able to motivate her. More than just the physical action, potty training is a lot of mental readiness and preparation.

This book is a comprehensive potty training guide to help parents get through the process seamlessly. It covers everything parents would want to know about potty training, including the methods used, nighttime potty training, training multiples and children with special needs, how to know it's the right time, and common dilemmas parents face.

You may feel you are in a dilemma. You want to start potty training your child but don't know when to start or how to do it. That's okay my friend, you are a single dad, and it is your first time. All these feelings are natural. I will help you understand what the process entails and empower you with the skills you need to potty train your child. The idea is that every child is like a snowflake, meaning the process will be unique for each child. By the time you are done with the book, you should be able to tailor the tips I have provided here to match your child's unique needs.

If you feel anxious, since you are a single parent and do not know how to hack potty training, then the tips I give in this book will surely help your child and you as well. You are earnestly trying to help your child learn independence, but the task seems too overwhelming for you. I understand that; I have been there too, but the entire journey is about patience and readiness. Do not lose faith!

Moreover, you may have tried potty training but failed miserably in the past, so you have turned to this book for some help. I will provide you with surefire tips to ensure success in your next trial. I will also be providing solutions to some of the challenges you could have experienced during the potty-training process. I am a father to three angels, and I have 10+ years of experience in the field of parenting. I want to share that with my fellow fathers.

Between caring for my beautiful daughters and working hard to provide for them, my fatherhood journey has not been an easy one. Along the way, I learned several hacks that made parenting easier for me, and I want to share my experience with you to ensure you are equipped with the necessary knowledge to tackle the challenges of fatherhood.

Potty training is one of the hardest parts of raising a toddler. Eventually, you must wean children off diapers, and knowing when or how to do this doesn't come naturally to all parents. By sharing my experiences and lessons I have learned, I believe this book will be a game-changer for many dads and moms out there. Finally, helping you potty train your little one matters deeply to me because I understand the importance of training children to be independent.

You could fall within any of the following categories:

- fathers to toddlers.
- mothers looking for answers
- teachers of preschoolers
- daycare center teachers

- a parent to your first child
- a parent to a boy or a girl

You could be living anywhere in the world, but we all have one common denominator—potty training. Who would have thought?

I want to present you with the opportunity of learning directly from my experiences of potty training my daughters. I have spent two years collecting information and research on potty training, and I have compiled it for you to have all the knowledge in one place. There will be numerous tips, new solutions, and personal stories which will help you get through this phase. By the end of this book, you will have learned the following:

- cognitive, psychological, and emotional growth patterns to look out for when gauging whether your children are ready for potty training
- the stages and potty-training methods to consider for your children
- tips for ensuring you have a successful potty-training experience
- what nighttime potty training entails and how to do it
- how to potty train a child with special needs
- the tips for potty training multiples

- answers to common dilemmas parents face
- courage to potty train your children successfully

I will also provide access to a cheat sheet detailing all the items you need to potty train your children.

So, my friends, let's get going! I wish you the best of luck in your endeavors.

1

GETTING STARTED

As a single father, when Mia finished potty training, I was over the moon. I did a little dance with her because I could not contain my excitement. You might think there are bigger joys in life, but when you are a parent—especially a single father—this is a big accomplishment.

As a parent, you will be delighted to see your child successfully conclude the toilet-training process. No more loading your grocery cart with diapers (at least for this child), and accidents have declined to a manageable few, phew! However, the most important factor of completing toilet training is that by learning to control this bodily function, your child has moved significantly closer toward self-mastery, which is every young child's goal, as well as a parent's goal.

Each time you encourage your child to use the toilet "like a grown up," your little one is practicing their new skill, and succeeding repeatedly gives them a wonderful new sense of competence and independence. The feeling of successfully completing a challenge will add to your child's confidence in other areas of their life, including social and academic pursuits. It is important to recognize the level of accomplishment your toilet trained child has reached, even if there is an occasional accident.

During parenthood, it is fascinating to discover our own long-unexamined assumptions and buried emotions as we interact with our children. When your child was first born, you may have been surprised at how you responded to each new experience. You may have been awed or frightened by the act of childbirth, anxious about the journey, and confident or nervous the first time you held your child.

Similarly, toilet training has been known to surface unconscious buried feelings such as competitiveness, anxiety, anger, neediness, and ambition amongst others.

(American Academy of Pediatrics, 2009). Whether reasonable or not, it is not always possible to rationalize your feelings. When introspecting on the emotional responses you experienced while toilet training your children, think about why your emotions were stirred by these specific situations and whether you found a positive way to express them. Your emotions may range from positive to regret. By thinking about why you're feeling certain emotions and what you did about them, you can learn a lot about yourself and apply them to other parenting situations. This really helps for single-father parenting as well because it brings a lot of things into perspective.

Toilet training—a valuable task—has greater value in teaching parents more about their children, themselves, and their dynamics as a family. Ideally, you would be able to draw upon your experiences while toilet training, as you move forward in your single father journey, to further effective communication, promotion of desirable behavior, positive approach to new challenges, and easy toilet training of future children.

Toilet training not only helps you achieve better insight into your emotions but also the psyche of your child. Looking back at the experience you are better able to discern what works best for your child—setting a schedule for them or allowing them to pick the right time. Do they respond better to rewards or words of appreciation?

As a single father, you might observe that using positive reinforcement, such as love, praise, and rewards, is a powerful motivator for your child to succeed and speaks to their desire to please you. Using these positive reinforcements can help your child achieve academic, social, and personal success as they move from kindergarten to higher grades and even later in their lives.

Toilet training also provides great insight into your family dynamics. Over the course of the 6 months or more that it takes, you will be able to observe the different roles you and your partner play in child raising. One might be the "disciplinarian" while the other may be more permissive; one might be more willing to do things for the child, while the other might push the child to be more independent. While one parent might be the person the child approaches in the case of an accident, the other might be the parent the child announces their success to. This challenging time can also be a good indicator for when one of you has reached their limit and need an intervention from the other.

These dynamics hold true even in two-household families. However, if you are a single or divorced father, you will most probably play both roles in your child's life when they are with you, and you will have to find a balance in your approach.

Some of the patterns formed during these years might continue well into your child's life into adulthood. However, as parents, you must also recognize that as your child grows, some of these patterns may switch, and some might be abandoned completely. The key thing to remember is that your child is developing a separate relationship with both of his parents, and this is part and parcel of the child growing up and becoming themselves.

Insights about your parenting style that you gain during this time can be further used to make changes where necessary. In acknowledging your different parenting styles and finding a viable compromise within a two-household family, you don't undermine each other's efforts. Instead, it gives your child the chance to see multiple strategies used to accomplish the same goal. This allows your child room to make mistakes and learn from them. You may even find it helpful to speak with your child to see if there is a technique that makes them feel better or worse, thereby helping you mold your style to one that works better for them.

Once your child has achieved this developmental milestone, as a family, you all can feel proud of completing a major parenting challenge. Experiencing the pleasure of achieving a goal will make future successes more likely and make your parenting unit ready for future challenges. While there might be accidents in the future, it is important to appreciate the success of this milestone which has helped your child become more confident, independent, and have more pride in their ability to master new skills.

When Mia did complete her potty training, apart from our little celebratory dance, we ordered in pizza and watched her favorite cartoon—*Frozen*. Celebrating with Mercy and Ava just made it all the merrier, and everyone was able to partake in the happiness of the event.

BEFORE YOU BEGIN

As a single father, potty training your children may feel daunting because you may feel like you are not in control of the situation and changing diapers may feel like added stress. If there is one thing true about potty training, it is that you have very little control, but everything is (for the most part) contained. You might also feel like you "just can't do it anymore" throughout the process but remember that that feeling is completely normal. Fear not, here are some tips on how to best prepare for potty training your little ones. Don't worry, potty training may disrupt your toddler's schedule and your life, but it does so for a short time only. With these tips, you will feel better prepared.

- **Choose a Method:** You've undoubtedly already done some research on toilet training and might or might not have chosen a technique. It is recommended to select a method unless you're one of those parents who have incredible intuition and just 'know' what they are doing. No matter what method you choose, there will come a point where you might find yourself wondering what you're doing and need some form of guidance at some time.
- **Be Prepared:** It is always good to be prepared for everything, and potty training is no different. The truth is, you may have no idea how things will turn out, so planning for the worst-case scenario is a great first step. Be sure to stock up on helpful items that support your chosen method.
- **Take a Break:** With potty training, you're in it for the long haul. Remember to take a well-deserved break. When your child goes down for a nap or quiet time, do something that relaxes you. Take up offers from anyone willing to relieve you for a while. Keep in mind that both you and your child will be psychologically

exhausted by potty training, so taking a break is very important!

- **Be Mindful of Your Child's Emotions:** Mercy was our first born, and her personality was a lot like mine. She likes things to be done in a particular way, and she always tries to live up to my expectations. During the first week of potty training, her behavior was terrible. Fortunately, I was able to take a step back and see what it really was—frustration. Rather than be overly strict with her, scheduling extra hugs, stories, and fun times boosted her self-confidence and she began to take down the toilet.

- **Avoid Comparison:** No two children are the same, and it is unfair to compare your child to others as it raises unrealistic expectations. Children can be potty trained using various methods because different children may have different needs and personalities. Children will learn how to use the toilet on their own, and it may not be easy, but they will make it in their own time. Most importantly, don't pay too much attention to other parents talking about how soon their kids trained themselves!

- **Mentally Prepare and Stay Strong:** When I decided it was time to teach Mia how to use the bathroom, I had to mentally prepare for the job.

I reminded myself that accidents happen, and any type of training takes time and patience. "We can do it, just stay strong," I told myself as I prepared to get rid of the diapers and start potty training over a long weekend. "Don't give up no matter how bad it gets."

- **Fear Not:** The problem with fear is that it usually grows from small, often illogical, seeds of doubt. Your brain can take over and turn things into much bigger problems or worries. At first, you think that you know what you're doing, but then your toddler does the exact opposite of what you have asked. It is easy to fall into the trap of thinking it is your fault or that you are doing something wrong. Don't!

MY EXPERIENCE

The first day (I began on a Thursday) of potty training with Mia as a single father was not the best, but that was expected. By the end of it, I was tired but still hoping for a breakthrough. Friday came and went with lots of mishaps and no triumphs. By Saturday, my uneasiness over the entire process had only grown. Between bouts of crying (I felt like an awful parent for making her go through this), I cleaned up pee and waited for a sign that Mia was getting the hang of it.

By day four—the conclusion of our long weekend—I couldn't do anything but attempt to keep my brain calm. I took a long shower and attempted to decompress. Still, I was troubled. "She'll never get it," I cried to my mother. "We wasted a lovely holiday weekend, and my daughter will wear diapers forever." She assured me that the situation would get better, and my child would eventually understand. Unfortunately, anxiety doesn't mix well with uncertainty, and I needed to know when. That's not how raising a little child works, especially when you are a single parent.

Finally, the day came when I watched as my child suddenly stopped playing with her toys, strolled over to her potty, and peed. It was as if a light bulb went on in her head, and all of a sudden, she caught on. My uneasiness melted...slightly.

REMEMBER

Learning to use the potty continued to be an ongoing process for Mia, and when I look back on those minutes of crippling anxiety, I wonder why I was so stressed over the fact of her not being able to do it. In case you ever feel the same way—stressed that you'll come up short at potty-training your child—the following master tips can help.

- **Plan Ahead:** Since chaos can make an on-edge individual more stressed, choosing how you will potty train before you begin is key in helping everybody remain calm. Begin by perusing books or articles and picking the strategy you need to follow—keeping in mind that there's no one "right" approach. My ex-wife and I tried the "naked weekend" approach with Ava. In this method, you clear your calendar and spend a few days letting your child run around in the buff with the potty at center stage.
- **Remain Calm:** The most important thing is to be prepared and flexible. If the parent is potty training with a sense of urgency, stress, or doubt, then even the most eager child will pick up on these feelings of anxiety and stress. I like to tell parents to take a breath with each word because it calms things down and helps you speak in slower tones. This way, you do not end up sounding shrill and high-pitched when talking to your little one. Moreover, I propose downloading a breathing and contemplation app on your phone. Centered breathing can ease uneasiness and let you calmly address what's going on in the situation at hand.
- **Seek Help:** Another thing to remember is to

keep your resources handy. Tips and tricks can be found in training materials, like a book, that backs the potty-training strategy you're utilizing.

Remember my friend, getting started is the first step—one you need to take with patience and preparation. Once you've potty train your child successfully, you can enjoy your self-sufficient toddler. They won't need your help every time they go to the toilet, and this will be very liberating for you both.

2

PERFECT TIMING

Once you have made ample preparation, mentally and physically, you will have to start looking at whether your child is ready or not because, well, the process won't be complete without them!

WHEN SHOULD POTTY TRAINING START?

The most common question among new parents is what age and time is right to potty train your child? Is it better to start early, or should you wait? The best answer to this question is that you should start potty training your child when they are ready and show positive signs—not before that.

Most children are not ready to be potty trained until they are at least 18 months of age (*Average Age for Potty*

Training Boys and Girls, 2018) . A healthy child needs to be both emotionally and physically ready for this, and most children usually reach this stage between the ages of 18 months to 3 years. Boys tend to take longer than girls to be ready for potty training. Most parents start the training within this window, but to be honest, there no set ages at which the process needs to start. Therefore, parents should not force their children to start before they are ready.

Different cultures around the world have different parenting traditions and norms. In some parts of the world, parents start potty training their child as early as four to five months old. This is a method called elimination communication. The parents start monitoring the child for signs the infant needs to go to the potty and rushes them to the bathroom to use the potty. However, this method is discouraged by experts as the child is too young, and this may cause problems later in life. Parents also must realize that each child is different, and for each child, the potty training pattern and timing will be different. So, be patient my friend.

Children under 2 years of age cannot control their bladder, and their rectum isn't mature enough to control when they poop. True independence is a lot to ask of a baby, as it means that they know how to:

- use the toilet
- hold it until they reach the toilet
- flush
- pull their clothes up and down
- wipe their bottom without your help

All of this does not happen in most children until the age of about three or four years. This is regardless of when you start potty training or the method you choose to follow.

Potty training a child is one of the most tedious jobs that a parent will ever have. It is one of the most non-glamorous tasks of all the parenting responsibilities, but it is something that everyone needs to do as part of child rearing. It is an aspect that all parents must learn and manage.

Like many parts of parenting, potty training is also especially difficult for first time parents and single parents. However, there are various tried and tested techniques and methods available, which makes it easier to for caregivers and parents. It is essential to know when to start the process of potty training a child to make the work easier on both parties. Be on the lookout for the following signs that may signal your child is ready to begin this new phase of life:

- Your child has a set pattern and timing for pooping.
- Your child will give signs and clues when they are going to poop. These include signs such as holding or touching their diaper, bending forward, or crouching down.
- Your child will look for a private space or have a secluded corner where they go when they are about to poop.
- Your child is uncomfortable and wants a diaper change after pooping.

Even when you are observing all the cues and are confident about potty training, you shouldn't drive your child towards potty training if the following situations or changes are taking place:

- any major change in the family dynamics (birth of a sibling, etc.)
- a change of space or moving into a new house or room
- admission in day care or preschool
- changes in your child's habits or routines
- sickness

Potty Training at Age 2

After your child turns 2, they will start noticing your daily patterns and may observe you use the potty. This might lead them to take an interest in being potty trained. You must take advantage of this interest and your child's readiness and introduce the use of the potty to them.

When Ava turned two-years-old, I started noticing that she was very curious whenever Mercy would use the potty in the morning. A few days into this observation, I noticed that Ava could be found around the potty area whenever she would need to potty or pee. One day she got really excited after Mercy was done using the potty. She wanted to sit on it, and so she tried climbing up. My ex-wife and I looked at her in amazement. But we understood the cue and helped Ava up and made her sit on the potty. Ava did the same for the next few days, and this started her potty-training process.

Two-year-old children are quick to pick up new habits and are in a development phase where they will quickly adapt to potty training, so strike while the iron is hot.

Potty Training at Age 3

Children are usually ready by age 3 to be fully potty trained. So if your child has hit this mark, get going. However, do know that some children might need extra time and may take another 6 to 7 months to get ready.

Potty Training at Age 4

Most children are usually fully potty trained by age 4. However, some might still be struggling with the process. If your child is still wetting their pants with pee or poop more than three to four times in a week, then it would be wise to consult your child's pediatrician. An expert opinion is always welcomed.

Although every parent wants to potty train their child at the earliest and in the shortest time frame possible, you should not force your child into jumping on the bandwagon as soon as possible. Each child is different and has a different learning pace. Parents should look for signs that a child is ready and then start the process. It is also important to remember that potty training is a lengthy process, and it usually takes about 8 to 10 months to complete. You will need to be patient with your child, respect their boundaries and limitations, and only then will the process go smoothly.

Because you are a single father, you will have more challenges to face since you are alone. So, practice some self-care in the form of:

- patience for yourself
- self-love
- reaffirming positive talk

EMOTIONAL GROWTH NEEDED FOR TOILET TRAINING

Besides a child's physical and mental growth, a child's emotional readiness is also important for potty training. Reading emotional cues can be the most difficult task particularly as at this age children experience a wide array of emotions. Emotional issues can be quite problematic in potty training especially for children who like to assert their free will and independence. Children at this stage are also testing the rules and have a desire of self-mastery and controlling their environment.

It is important for you to observe your child's emotional state before introducing them to potty training. You must consider your child's general behavior at home and their behavior when introduced to the idea of potty training. If your child is generally responsive towards potty training and enjoys the steps involved, consider that as an upward trajectory towards self-mastery of their training.

If your child is non-responsive and generally uncomfortable, then you might be facing a conflict and would need to be more patient. You might even decide to look for a better time to train your child. You may think, "how can my toddler know any better for themselves?" But believe me, they do.

Self-Mastery

As human beings we are all continuously evolving and trying to be a better version of ourselves. This is something that starts in our childhood. A child desires to be a master of their own body and starts craving independence to be a master of their environment as early as 18 months or so.

This kind of ambition is great for introducing potty training as your child will try to act like a big kid and mimic the behavior of older children around them. However, this also has the potential of working negatively since children's desires to be independent may propel them to make decisions which cannot be controlled by their developing body.

You may need to be careful as to how you introduce potty training to your child. Your child may resist the process altogether because they are establishing their own privacy and independence. Your child may also run off and scream out "no," to show their independence. This may negatively impact potty training process as your child is tempted to get off the potty and run away to prove their independence. This may also result in accidents. The more attention you pay to such experiments the more the child will tend to repeat them.

It is best that you treat these incidents as normal occurrences and do not pay much attention to them. Wait for a little while until your child is a bit more mature. As with most aspects of parenting, potty training also needs to be done with a lot of patience and the right timing.

Resistance

For any kind of learning to take place, your child will need a safe environment and will need to be in their comfort zone to learn any new skills. Similarly, any change in the environment or any major change in your child's life can have an adverse effect on their learning. For example, a change of residence, addition of a new sibling, or parents separating are all instances which can adversely affect children and upset them. They may react by trying to gain tighter control over aspects within their reach, one of these could be a resistance to potty training.

Resistance is the result of children trying to take control of their personal aspects. Older toddlers who may have some control over their bladder and bowel movements may hold it in longer in their attempts to resist parents' potty training efforts. Your child may get constipated because of this reluctance and resistance to parental pressure. The best way to tackle this is to comfort your child and speak to them about what is upsetting them and to give them more time to face the situation. With help from parents, children will soon move through this stage and be ready to tackle potty training once again. Treat your child with respect and remember communication is key—even for toddlers!

Desire for Approval

Children start seeking their parent's approval as early as their first birthday and maybe even before. You will notice this change in your child as they begin to understand the idea of cause and effect relationships. They learn what kind of behavior and actions get them a positive affirmation such a small cuddle, a hug, or love from a parent and which actions prompt such reactions. Furthermore, your child becomes curious to know which action will receive which type of reaction, and so the testing begins.

I was always flabbergasted when 18-month-old Mercy would try a new trick to gain my attention in different ways. Sometimes she would pull my hair, pull my nose, or sometimes just poke me to get reactions out of me. She would then wait for my reaction to understand whether this was something I liked or disliked.

Similarly, when Ava reached this age, she started mimicking Mercy whenever she would sit on the potty by sitting like her. That was when I decided to take advantage and used these examples to initiate Ava's potty training. I made sure to reward Ava for her good behavior each time she achieved something. By rewards I don't mean buying an expensive toy or an extravagant outing but rather smaller rewards such as words of affirmation, praise, or extra play time. Because by this point, Ava—like many other children her age—could effectively gauge which actions garnered praise and which did not. Hence, when you praise and reward your child for the smallest success in the process of potty training, they will most likely repeat it.

Two best tools available for parents to take advantage of during the potty-training process are the child's need to be appreciated and the child's ability to imitate actions of people around them. Therefore, throughout the potty-training process, appreciating small achievements will make it easier for your child to learn.

As your child grows older, even if they are not completely potty trained, they will have a renewed desire to please you which can be easily achieved through the process of potty training.

Social Awareness

As children grow older, they develop an increased affinity toward observing and being like others around them. This keeps increasing as toddlers start preschool and begin interacting with other children. At eighteen months, a child will likely be fascinated with other children around them and will start mimicking their behavior. This interest in imitating their peers may lead to your child wanting to potty train as other kids around them may already be using the potty. What parent would not want this? Parents can also motivate their children by casually pointing out the children who are wearing big kid underwear and using the potty. Believe me when I say big kid underwear is a big deal in this age group. It is akin to getting your driver's license for teenagers.

As your child grows and reaches two-and-a-half years of age, they will begin to differentiate between genders and will start imitating the ways of the same sex parent. Parents can use this time to allow their child to observe the same sex parent while they use the toilet to satisfy the child's curiosity. This also demonstrates the basic concepts/use of a toilet which satisfies another curiosity in most children. However, if you are a single father like I am and do not have the same sex as your child to imitate, worry not! Mia has two elder sisters who she observed. If it wasn't for her sisters, I would ask my mother and so on. Remember to ask for support whenever you feel stuck; you are not alone!

PSYCHOLOGICAL READINESS AND MOTOR SKILLS NEEDED FOR TOILET TRAINING

Parents are very familiar with the routine of feeding infants. As soon as you are done feeding your baby formula or breast milk, it seems they need a diaper change. This cycle of feeding and changing occurs so quickly in infants that it can be used as a perfect example of what is going in at one end comes out on the other end. This process usually happens because the baby's digestive system is not fully formed and strong enough at this stage.

It is important to understand your child's digestive system. Your child's bladder and intestines are small, and their sphincter muscles are not strong enough to keep the bladder and rectum closed. Therefore, babies are fast in passing urine and poop. This process remains involuntary until the baby is at least 18 months old, and until that time, a baby cannot be potty trained.

Awareness of the Need to Go

Your child's body will begin to develop by the time they reach the milestone of their first birthday. At this point, your child starts feeling the sensations of a full bladder and a full rectum, a sign that your child needs to pee or poop. This is a sensation that your child needs to recognize before potty training. In most cases, children will show awareness of this to the parents or caregivers by signals such as squatting and grunting or touching the diaper area. These behaviors show that the child might be feeling the need to relieve themselves.

Once these signals are in place, it is a good idea to start connecting the feeling of fullness or the need to poop and pee with the act of going potty. This can be done in multiple ways by parents and caregivers. For example, once you see that child is about to poop or pee, you can comment saying, "Hey, I think someone needs to go poopy," or "Little baby needs to go toilet, do you feel you need to?"

For me, with my three daughters, potty training was a struggle, and I had to try various strategies. The idea of potty training is a lot like the carrot and stick theory. For every good action, your child needs to be rewarded to reinforce the action. For example, if your child dirtied their diaper, the diaper needs to be changed promptly to reinforce the concept that poop and pee should be removed from the body and discarded, and they must be cleaned after that.

Parents need to remain positive throughout the process of potty training. Negative words and actions should be completely avoided and replaced with only positive words and actions around potty time. The aim is to instill in your child the awareness and knowledge of the need to go to the toilet for both poop and pee. Then, they can build on this awareness when the time comes for potty training.

Motor Skills

Your child is growing day by day, and their body muscles are developing and getting strong enough to perform daily tasks. Keep in mind that the development of your child's motor skills up to a certain level is also an important consideration before you start potty training your child.

Some of the important skills that are useful, if developed, are the ability to walk, the ability to talk, and the ability to follow instructions. The ability to walk is the most obvious motor skill that, if developed, can be the most useful for potty training children, as they can walk to the potty themselves, without assistance.

Most children have developed the ability to walk by the age of one. As your child reaches the eighteen-month mark, other motor skills are also developing or improving gradually. This includes the child's ability to talk and use more words to describe what their need is. Furthermore, the use of their limbs and hands gives them the ability to handle their clothes for dressing and undressing.

Parents can also take advantage of motor skills development by teaching children new things such as dressing and undressing themselves or by reading them interactive books while they are waiting to go to the potty or pooping. Their patience will develop over time.

The development of these motor skills will make your child more confident and aide in your journey of potty training.

COGNITIVE AND VERBAL SKILLS NEEDED
FOR TOILET TRAINING

There are some skills, which once mastered, stay with you for a lifetime. Remember the first time you tried to learn how to ride a bicycle. Do you recall the first trip to Walmart to buy a bicycle with training wheels? What about the first time your dad helped you with the ride? Learning to keep the bike stable and balanced and learning to pedal was a process. As time passed, you grew more proficient and the wheels came off. Do you remember the feeling as you zipped around on your bicycle across town? This skill is one that stays with you no matter how much time passes by.

It's the same process and learning curve for your child during the potty-training process. Your child needs to learn to coordinate all the complex physical and cognitive tasks that go with it. They must familiarize themselves with all parts of their body and their functions, develop awareness of associating the physical sensation of the need to go to the potty, and connect this function with their physical body parts.

Then, your child needs to learn to get to the potty, get on top of it, and sit patiently through the process of it. Through the learning process, your child will need to understand the need, the commands, and the body responses.

Body Awareness

The most important aspect to consider when deciding if your child is ready for potty training is their body awareness. For potty training, your child must know and understand what a full bladder feels like and what happens as a result of this feeling. This usually happens at around the age of twelve to eighteen months.

As your child grows older, their body awareness will grow. For example, your child will begin to show discomfort after they have soiled their diaper or in extreme cases try to remove it. By age two, children are very aware of their body and are quite interested in their body parts. This is the age when they start talking about their private parts and like to be free of any clothes. This interest indicates that a child is open to learning how the body works and about private body parts and their use. It is also around the same time that the child starts to learn through their own experiences. Therefore, just sitting on the potty until they naturally release is also a lesson in itself.

This process, followed by positive affirmation from a parent, works really well. All these actions help the child connect the object (toilet) with an action (elimination).

Making Plans and Following Through

It is important to understand the connection between the desire to eliminate and the actual action of pooping or peeing. This is a crucial first step towards toilet training for your child. Even so, your child will need more practice before they imagine themselves on the toilet whenever they need to go. This involves planning how they will get to the bathroom to go and remembering their plan long enough to carry it out. They must master the ability to visualize activities (symbolic cognition), plan for execution (problem solving), and remember and retain. These abilities emerge at the age of one year in children but become much more established by the age of two or more.

The correlation between remembering and doing is important for a child to execute their potty routine. The ability to think of an absent object (recall from memory) starts developing in your child by one year of age. The earliest sign of this is your child crying when you leave the room. It is because your child can now picture you and know you exist but are just out of sight. As your child grows, your child's motor skills start developing, so they can reach you wherever you are. Similarly, at the right potty-training age, your child can recall the potty when needed and walk to it for use.

By the age of two, your child may be picturing their toilet whenever they want to go to the bathroom. They could even be able to locate the potty when they need it. However, they may still need your assistance in making the connections necessary and following through before other thoughts or occurrences distract them.

Your child's growing interest in problem solving around the age of two-and-a-half or three will help them complete the sequence of tasks involved with potty training independently. Solving difficulties necessitates seeing a solution and devising a strategy to reach it. Watching your child develop these abilities is one of the most rewarding signs that he or she is on the verge of toilet-training readiness.

From getting their toy car back from another child during playtime to negotiating an extra piece of cake after dinner, you'll see your child solve issues all day long as they approach their third birthday. Your child's ability to plan how they get their desired wish/object is a solid indicator that they are also cognitively competent enough to keep dry without diapers and be potty trained.

REMEMBER

As your child reaches the three-year mark, their motor and cognitive skills are more focused and developed. They are now better at focusing and resisting distraction on the way to the task at hand. Your child must have also started communicating and using sentences. They will be able to communicate any problem they may experience or any fears that they may have developed to ask for your help.

These critical cognitive and linguistic changes, which are just as necessary for toilet training success as physical growth, are why most parents believe that starting training at the age of two-and-a-half or three makes the process much simpler. Waiting for your child's natural development to fall into place is a wise decision, especially if you've started laying the framework at a younger age.

Remember to follow your child's lead rather than forcing them to be ready when you are.

3

THE STAGES AND METHODS

There are various methods that we, as parents, can use to potty train our little ones.

I will describe several of them comprehensively to help you make an informed decision regarding the most suitable method for your child. Remember that one method won't work for all your children. I used three different methods for my three daughters.

THE STAGES

Before we go in depth on the different methods of training, it is beneficial to understand the four basic stages of potty training.

▶ **Stage One: Toilet Play**

- Your baby is used to going potty with their clothes on.
- They usually see others using the toilet.
- After all this observation, they are keen to try using the toilet.

▶ **Stage Two: Toilet Practice**

- Your child has gone through stage 1.
- They start using the toilet properly.
- They are learning to wash their hands.
- Your child realizes whether their diaper is wet or dry.

▶ **Stage Three: Toilet Learning**

- Your child starts wearing proper underwear instead of relying on diapers and learns how to express themselves and hold their urine for a longer period.
- They wish to stay clean.
- They learn proper words for using the toilet.
- They develop the ability to pull their pants up and down when using the toilet.

- For proper bowel movement, they learn to concentrate and push the stool out.
- At times when forgetting to use the toilet, they are able to express that their diapers are wet and need to be changed.

▶ **Stage Four: Independent Toileting**

POTTY TRAINING: WHICH METHOD IS BEST?

For each method in this section, I am going to discuss:

- the definition
- who uses it
- how it works (the process/steps)
- pros and cons

There are many different opinions concerning what age parents should start the toilet training process for their child. Also, every parent is likely to have their own training method which may be different from yours. There is no right fit for everyone.

The parent, by demonstrating how to use the toilet himself in front of the child, may be the best way to initiate the training process. There are many ways a parent can develop the child's interest in using the toilet. Such as:

- speaking to their children on how to use the toilet properly and asking them regularly if they need to go to the bathroom
- treating the child to their favorite meal or awarding them with a gold star to develop the child's interest in the toilet training process
- using immersion training to achieve the necessary results from their child in a brief period of, say, two weeks
- letting the child become accustomed to toiled training over a prolonged period to put less stress on the child

All the methods described above can provide the desired results for your child. However, it should be noted that it is better not to stick with just one technique, but instead you should try out a combination. Trying to understand your child's preferable style will yield a much easier experience. This will also help you get to know your child in a better way and make your child more receptive towards you.

THE 3-DAY METHOD

There is no doubt that the benefits of getting your child out of diapers in just three days are aplenty. How amazing does it sound? Three days and you are done potty training your child for life! Unbelievable.

If this method works, there can be numerous benefits like using less diapers, saving money, and cutting down on landfill waste. When using cloth diapers instead of disposable diapers, a lot can be saved on laundry expenses as well. What a dream come true, especially for a single father!

People who are experts in potty training agree that potty training should be conducted in a less stressful environment for the child. They should not fear being rebuked or humiliated by you for any mistake during the use of the toilet. When these mistakes happen, it is advisable that you carry your child to the potty and remind them where they must direct the poop or pee.

Before You Begin

There are various opinions of experts as to what the most suitable age is for children to start potty training. One such expert named Jensen believes that 22 months is the proper age for children to start potty training (*Potty Train in 3 Days*, 2016). Another expert and originator of the revered *Diaper Free Toddlers* program, Julie Fellom, feels that between 16 and 26 months is the ideal period to start your child's potty training.

There are differing opinions that girls are easier to potty train than boys, but it really depends on your child and their ability to learn in a short period of time. It has no relation to the sex of your child. Neuberger feels that during the potty-training process it is better for both the girls and boys to sit down on the toilet while peeing or pooping. Neuberger feels that once children have passed stool sitting down on the toilet for about 10 times, they can then be encouraged as a second step to start peeing while standing up. In this case the parents may also assist them by standing up with their child.

For a successful three-day potty-training program, you must prepare. The most important thing in the three-day training program is the potty chair. There are different expert opinions on whether it is necessary to have one potty chair or two. For example, Jensen feels having just one potty chair will get your child better accustomed to using the same chair, instead of two different ones which might confuse them. Fellom, on the other hand, is of the opinion that potty chairs placed all around the house will encourage children to use any one of them when needed.

Size is also relevant. Neuberger is of the opinion that a floor level potty chair will be more comfortable for to use as their feet can be closer to the floor. This will greatly help your child's pelvic area, and they will learn the correct sitting position.

In a three-day training program, it is important that your child should be fed salty foods, popsicles, and watermelons, which are a diuretic, and can induce frequent urination. It is also important that you should stay at home and nearby a toilet for the entire time to properly monitor the progress.

There is also the concept of rewards for to encourage their interest in potty training. Jensen suggests using encouraging items like stickers, small toys, or treats as rewards. Other experts do not agree on this approach. Fellom is totally opposed to this kind of approach as she feels that your child should develop their own interest without any kind of motivation or reward.

When it comes to underwear, you should be aware of how many pairs need to be kept at hand, depending on the frequency of your child's bowel habits. Jensen feels that up to 20 to 30 pair per day should be stocked and ready for use. Others suggest the process of changing underwear should be at the end of the 3-day training period. Fellom is of the opinion that parents should wait 3 months before switching completely to underwear. There are other experts who feel that diapers, pull up pants, or even padded underwear should be avoided at all costs while starting the three-day potty-training program.

According to Fellom's advice, to start the 3-day training program, you should take compete rest by sleeping in on Wednesday, Thursday, and Friday. This will ensure that you are fresh and ready to start the 3-day training program. Without this proper rest, you may not be in position to pay full attention to your child for this specific program.

The Process

It is important to be steady and consistent. It is also vital for you to assess your home space and what would be a suitable option—space wise—to start the 3-day program. You will need to make the environment more conducive for your child in the weeks leading up to your attempt.

The first day of the program is by far the most crucial. During this time, you are required to monitor your child the entire day. Please make sure that you have carried out all household chores, before starting with day 1. Also, avoid using the phone as this may be an added distraction.

Your child should do away with the use of diapers, and you should throw away all the remaining diapers. This way, they will understand that you are discouraging the use of diapers, and this will also help you avoid temptation to fall back on the use of diapers as an aid for your child.

Your child should roam around in just their underwear and shirt during this program. As an alternative, you could allow your child to go completely bottomless for the first day (as some experts recommend). However, if it is cold, your child can roam around wearing just a sweater and socks but no underwear or pants. We don't want our children to become icicles.

It is imperative that your child's actions and behavior are closely monitored, and if they show any signs of beginning to pee or poop, you should usher them to the bathroom. Rest assured parents, while keeping a close eye on your child, you can continue with their normal house activities if you choose to.

As soon as you notice that your child is ready to pee or poop, you should take them straight to the bathroom and make it clear to them that the pee or poop should go straight into the potty. Every time your child gets even a drop of pee in the potty, they must be praised for their effort. Your child should be made to feel that it is a big event when they master the proper use of a toilet. While your child is using the toilet properly, you should do a silly or fun kind of potty dance for further encouragement. Whatever you do, make sure that it is exciting for them.

It is a good idea to frequently remind your child to go to the toilet to pee or poop. You can also check in regularly if your child's underwear is dry most of the time. If it is, make sure you applaud them. It may seem like a small feat for us, but it is quite a big deal for them.

Your child's performance should be monitored closely during the day. If you feel that your child has successfully been able to pee in the potty 10 to 12 times without your help, then they are almost ready to use the toilet all by themselves, without any help. Hoorah!

You will get an indication of whether your child is responding to the training or not on the very first day. If you feel your child is not using the potty properly and is resistant to the training, then maybe their body is not yet prepared for this. Neuberger feels that, in this case, your child's interest in the training process is lacking at this early stage, and their body is not ready for it. Do not get flustered and disappointed during this process and instead of making a big issue out of it, try again within a month or two.

According to Jenson, there is another option that can be tried by the parent to get the desired results. During the three-day period, in addition to training your child during the daytime, your child can also be made to get up in the night and pee. However, Neuberger feels that children are not mentally prepared for training in the night until they have completed at least three to six months of the daytime training. Many experts feel that nighttime is a totally different approach for your child and is a less emotional, more organic process. If you feel that you would prefer to let your child be diaper free during their sleep hours, make sure that they have limited amounts of liquid and go to the potty before sleeping.

On most occasions, your child adapts to using the toilet on the second and third day of training. They can communicate their need of going to the bathroom by speaking or through gestures. This is the time when they should be left alone to practice on their own. Let your child be on their own which will further bolster their confidence.

After the three-day **training program, experts are divided.** some experts feel that your child should start wearing underwear while other experts suggest your child should be pants free for at least a few weeks while they finish the process of potty training. According to Fellom, your child should roam around the house freely without their underwear for at least three months.

If your child is in a daycare center, stay in constant contact with your childcare provider and draw up a proper plan with them on how to manage your child. Fellom feels that children are very adaptable to any change of environment and don't really need the parent's guidance if they are well taken care of in the daycare center. However, it is important that they are comfortable with whatever system they are made to adopt at the day care center.

What if 3-Day Potty Training Doesn't Work?

If your child is unable to show any positive results in their 3-day potty training, this means that they are not ready and willing to undertake this daunting task at this tender age. If your child is among the relatively 7% who are unable to produce any results in the first attempt, wait six to eight weeks before giving it another try.

There could be certain medical reasons for your child's responsiveness. There may be issues such as emotional control, motor function responses, etc. Sometimes potty training can bring to the foreground hidden medical issues which need to be addressed by the parent at an early stage.

Flexibility on your part and not adhering to the training program (by constantly shifting between diapers and underwear) can be a deterrent for your child and may be counterproductive to the entire process. Parents are usually apprehensive, and children are very sharp and can sense their parent's anxiousness. Remember that your child has the capacity to feel your stress.

Even if the result of the 3-day potty program is not 100% satisfactory, my friend, do not be disheartened. Remember, there is also the possibility that even if your child has trained successfully within the 3-day training period, they are likely to have mishaps.

Moreover, since this method is hands on, it may be difficult for you as a single father. You need all the help you can get, not just with the potty-training process, but also household help.

CHILD-ORIENTED POTTY TRAINING

This method of potty training is more conducive for your child if they have not responded to any other training program.

The Steps of Child-Oriented Potty Training

Your child-oriented training program can be started when your child is 18 months old; this is the right age to introduce them to the potty. Your child should be made aware that the potty chair is special and solely belongs to them, and they should be made to realize that this special chair serves the same purpose as the toilet in the bathroom.

You should encourage your child to sit on the potty with their clothes on since this is the right way to introduce your child to sit on the potty. The clothes are necessary because we don't want our child to feel the coldness of the potty against their bare bottom, which is likely to deter them from using the potty. It would also be a good idea to read them a book of interest or promise them a reward. In this type of training, with your child's clothes on, they can get up from the potty any time they want to. It is less rigid.

If all goes well in the first stage, it is then time to make your child sit on the potty with their diaper off. This is just part of the practice for sitting on the potty. The actual peeing or pooping in the potty will come later as soon as your child is accustomed to sitting on the potty seat. If your child is still peeing and pooping in the diaper, it may be a wise idea for you to put the soiled diaper in the potty and then explain that the potty is the place where pee and poop should go, instead of the diaper.

The bare bottom usage of the potty by your child should be suggested to them each day. Repetition helps!

I became the king of repetition when I was solo training Mia. Your child should be reassured of their capabilities. Tell them, "You already know what to do in case you want to relieve yourself." Another tip that is helpful is to leave the potty seat around your child while they are playing or sitting. It just makes it convenient for them to access. Your child should be made aware of the potty from time to time, and if you feel that your child is showing any signs of readiness, then they should be guided to it as soon as possible. You can also introduce potty breaks for your child at regular intervals throughout the day.

Important Points About This Method

Ridiculing or punishing your child are not at all recommended. When you see your child using the potty all by themselves, you should praise them for their self-determination by using words of encouragement.

If you feel your child is not responding well to the training, it is advisable to step back. The basis of this method is that it opens avenues for an impassioned milestone of care and respect for your child. There are so many potty-training methods available. This makes it much easier for you to choose the best option most likely to suit your child in the best possible way.

Pros and Cons

The good thing about child-oriented potty training is that it makes it less stressful for your child. This method is generally pleasant for you both and avoids the hassles of more strict potty-training programs. Research indicates that many children have benefitted from this approach. It is also much easier for the parent to explain this method to their child. Also, with this kind of approach there is no need for the family members to alter their work schedules or take days off.

The drawback of this method is that it may take several months or more to produce the desired results, as compared to the faster and more rigid methods. It also depends on whether your child wants to use the potty on any particular day. If your child is ready for pre-school, then this may be an added stress for the parent, as the parent will need to meet a deadline to make your child diaper free before starting pre-school. Moreover, this approach may lack the ability to build your child's confidence to go to the bathroom and does not lead to developing your child's need to read their bodily signs when they need to go.

PARENT-LED POTTY TRAINING

If you are a working person and sticking to your work schedule is important for you, then this method is likely to appeal to you. The most appropriate age and time to implement this method is to observe when your child is showing signs of readiness.

This process is only workable if the parent or caretaker keep encouraging your child to use the toilet on a set schedule or give your child a certain timetable to adhere to for using the toilet. To make this approach successful it is advisable that your child is taken to the bathroom every 2 to 3 hours daily. As an alternative, your child should be told to use the toilet before or after every meal and also during their other activities and before going to sleep.

However, if your child feels that they need to use the toilet apart from the schedule laid out for them, please encourage it.

INFANT POTTY TRAINING

What is infant potty training? This is another term for "elimination communication" or "natural infant hygiene." Infant potty training requires that the baby is introduced to the toilet or potty at a very early age, normally between birth and 4 months.

Some parents who opt for this method do away with the use of diapers and prefer to rush the baby to the nearest bathroom whenever they foresee that the baby is ready to pee or poop. Some parents prefer to use diapers on their baby. In any case, by 18 months of training, most children have learned to use the toilet fully and can be considered successful in their training.

What are the Advantages of Infant Potty Training?

Scientifically there is very little data on infant potty training. However, many parents supportive of this program claim many advantages. There are many advantages of the infant training program. For example, it helps in developing a closer relationship and love between the parent and baby. It also makes the parent more aware of the baby's needs to pee or poop, as they are constantly being monitored.

The best advantage of this method is that it fosters a very close relationship with your child. It can be considered as a kind of conversation that you are having with your 3-month-old child. Bringing up a child by using this method also strengthens the use of the family bed instead of the baby cot, encourages breastfeeding by the mother, and requires carrying the baby close to you in your arms.

The use of this training method can also be very comfortable for the baby. Parents who use and support this type of training program, feel that babies usually cry and make a commotion because they have peed or pooped in their diaper, which makes them uncomfortable. Therefore, it is more advisable to let your child go diaper free.

The use of this method also allows your child to become more independent. As your child becomes more active and wants to be more independent, it can be much easier for the parent to inspire the baby to crawl to the potty or go to the toilet on their own. This practice will ultimately do away with the process of changing diapers all the time.

The use of this method also reduces diaper waste. As per the Environmental Protection Agency, a used diaper can be a serious environmental hazard since the used diapers can last for a very long period when disposed of as part of the garbage in the landfill. According to statistics, a baby goes through about 8,000 diapers in their early childhood. By using cloth diapers sparingly, it can greatly reduce the environmental impact as fewer resources will be required for washing the diapers daily. Reducing the use of diapers will not only be good for a cleaner environment, but also less financially stressful for the family.

Infant potty training is normal and natural. The mothers in Africa and Asia keep their bare bottomed infants clean as they manage to foresee when their child wants to pee or poop and keep the baby away from their bodies, so that the baby can relieve themselves. It would be safe to say that this method is both practical and workable, and copying and adapting this method by the parents in the western world is advisable.

What are the Disadvantages of Infant Potty Training?

Most experts are doubtful of using this method, as it involves too much effort on the part of many parents. This method can be very time consuming and may require a lot of commitment on part of the parent. Believers of infant potty-training method feel that you do not need to use this method around the clock. For example, it would be prudent to let your child roam around diaper free during a certain time of the day but only when you are at home. This technique may be used as often as possible to produce positive results.

The method of infant potty training can be very tough if both parents work full-time during the day. In this case, if the parents feel that the baby should be left at a daycare center, they should be aware that per licensing requirements of the daycare centers, they are not allowed to enlist an infant who has been trained to be diaper-less. Also, babysitters may be unwilling to handle this type of situation.

According to a study conducted by child development experts, as well as physicians at the American Academy of Pediatrics, your child may not be ready to be potty trained during their infancy. Babies are just beginning to become aware of the feeling of a full bladder or need to pass stool at about 12 months and can only develop moderate control of their bladder or bowel movement by the age of 18 months.

Toilet training can only bring about positive results when your child is mentally and physically developed to a certain extent. Potty training does not need to be a race with time, and starting an early potty-training program for your infant does not help your baby develop in other ways.

You should be prepared for mishaps during the potty-training process. Infant potty training is a very uphill task for the parent. Some babies tend to use the potty for a few weeks then revert to having periodic mishaps. Some other infants may completely stop having bowel movements and get constipated.

Parents should watch out for whether they are getting frustrated with their children. You must be patient and not get flustered if you feel that you are not getting the desired results from your children.

Proponents of this training method assert that this is less of a mess than the use of diapers. At the same time, you should be prepared with all cleaning materials for those occasions when your baby is unable get to the potty in time. There are many enzyme-based cleaners available in the market that are used for pets but can safely be used for cleaning human waste.

How can I get Started?

Those parents who have used this method of potty training recommend that it should be started between childbirth and 4 months. If you start the training program with an older child, it is more likely that they will take longer to learn, as they will have to unlearn their need and use of diapers.

Parents should observe their baby regularly to determine when the baby is ready to pee or poop. Kindly note if they are in the habit of going to the bathroom at a particular time, for example they may want to go right after waking up or maybe during the daytime. Notice if your child tries to make any visual communication, noises, or some unintelligible phrases which may indicate that they are ready to go to the toilet.

When you feel that your baby is making their usual sign to pee or poop, then you should carefully hold them over a potty. Try to introduce verbal communication with your child, like a sound, to which your child can get accustomed to when they are relieving themselves. I would advise you use this sound or phrase whenever you feel that your baby is ready to go to the bathroom. In case of any mishap while using the potty, you should treat it casually and be relaxed as this is a part of the potty-training process and mishaps will happen.

During the night, make sure that if your child is sleeping with you, a potty seat should be kept next to the bed, and your child should use the potty before going to bed. Some experts believe that babies seldom pee or poop during their deep sleep. However, if they do need to go, they will become restless or give an indication that they need to go to the potty. Other experts believe that the use of diapers at night is advisable. During the night, you can also use a waterproof mattress pad in case your child decides to pee or poop in the night during their sleep.

You need to be resilient during the training process. Please don't be a fuss pot while the potty-training process is underway. It is okay to use diapers sometimes, especially at night or when you are going out of the house. This can make life much easier for you. If possible, use cloth diapers. They are highly recommended by some experts because disposable diapers are very absorbent, and your baby may not be able to tell if they are wet or soiled.

WHAT YOU CAN DO

Following are some tips and tricks of the trade I will share with you:

- In this process, it is better to explain to your child that they will be taken to the toilet and how to use it properly. Your child should be introduced to wearing underwear and the parent should show your child that they are also wearing them. To pique your child's interest in using proper underwear, they can be introduced to TV characters like Batman, Spiderman, Barbie, or Elsa.
- To further develop your child's interest in using the toilet properly, they should be made to watch a parent or sibling using the toilet. As I have mentioned before, I made Mia observe Mercy and Ava.
- Your child should be given positive

encouragement for their effort.
- It is also a good idea to turn on the water tap during toilet training, which can be a source of guidance for your child.
- Try to develop your child's interest in reading books about toilet training.
- Your child should be made to realize that they are in full charge of the toilet training process and should be able to indicate to the parent when they are ready to go to the toilet.
- It would also be a good idea that when your child is using the toilet, there is a song playing. It just makes the process fun and entertaining.
- To attract your child's attention to using the toilet, you can use tactics like dancing or acting as an animal, being a goofball, or offering them books or toys to occupy them while sitting on the potty. Out of my three angels, Ava was the only one who loved reading on the toilet, while the other two preferred their toys.
- Please do educate your child about body parts and their functions. They do need to know what they are doing and why they are doing it.
- When you child is curious about something and wants to ask you questions, give them simple answers so that they are not embarrassed or

feel ashamed. It is, after all, a natural process which we all go through.
- After using the toilet, you must teach your child to wash their hands properly after every visit.
- Before going to sleep in the night, you should restrict your child's fluid intake.
- If your child does not pay any heed to the toilet training process, it should be delayed until such a time when they start taking an interest.
- Tell your child about the various items in the bathroom and what their functions are.
- To make your child feel more comfortable and confident, you should ask your child in a loving manner if they want to use the toilet many times in a day.
- Your child, if treated as an adult, will be more likely to indicate that they need to use the toilet all by themselves.
- Children should wear clothes that can be removed easily. The best suggestion would be to use sweatpants.

WHAT NOT TO DO

Following are some things which you should not be doing during the process of potty training your child:

- Do not make them wear fitted clothes.
- Do not scold and punish them for accidents.
- Children should not be encouraged to use the toilet for a period of more than five to seven minutes, otherwise they may begin to consider the bathroom environment as unpleasant, and this will backfire on the process of potty training.
- Do not force your child to be potty trained if they are not ready.
- Do not use negative words during the process.
- Do not use food or other treats as a bribe.
- Do not have unrealistic expectations.
- Do not compare.

It would not be strongly advisable for you to not compare your child with other children, especially their own siblings. I made it a point to do that with Mia. Since I was potty training alone, it was more challenging and at times frustrating, but I never let my frustration get the best of me. There were moments when I would think *why can't Mia be as quick as Mercy or as easy-going as Ava.* but I never voiced this out loud because all my daughters are unique and wonderful in their own ways.

HYGIENE

Following are some hygiene tips I would like to share with you:

- For girls, after using the toilet, they should be told to wipe from the front to the back; otherwise, there is a danger of getting bacteria from the anus into vaginal area.
- It is imperative that it should be instilled in your child to wash their hands thoroughly after using the bathroom.
- For your child to stay protected from any infection, they should be told to wipe themselves in a gentle way. This will also save them from any irritation in that area.
- If your child wets themself accidently, you should immediately change their clothes.

REMEMBER

There are various methods, and at the end of the day you should choose what you think works best for you and your child. Consider your schedule, your boundaries, your child's readiness, and their temperament. Then, pick which method you want to practice. For Mia, I opted for the child-oriented training method since I am a single father, and I needed to be flexible. Luckily, Mia responded well to it, and I also asked for help from my mother. When I would be at work, my mother would be at home with Mia to help her with potty training.

It took me around a month or so to finally have her fully and successfully potty trained. Be patient and remember it is not a race; it a process. Try out a few methods before sticking with the one that works best for you and your child.

In the next chapter, I will discuss how to prepare your child for the actual physical process of potty training.

4

DROPPING THE DIAPERS

Finally, the time has arrived. Regardless of your chosen method, you have reached the golden period of letting go off diapers. You will be overjoyed to realize that your child now needs fewer diaper changes. Within no time, you will also observe that your child is learning to stay dry during their sleep. This is a positive sign and shows that your child is ready for the commencement of dropping the diapers.

The most important part of attaining success in potty training is patience. Different approaches work for different children, but in general, the guidelines mentioned usually get the desired results you are seeking for your child.

The best news is that now, toward the end of this journey, the frequent use of diapers has drastically decreased. Also, your child's bowel movements will become more regular over time. It is also at this stage that your child may start disliking the use of diapers because they become stinky and filthy after being used. Consider it party time when your child starts disliking the use of stinky diapers.

As you near the end of your potty-training phase, know that you are not quite done. Don't forget that setbacks are possible. To avoid common pitfalls, I have a few pieces of advice I would like to share with you:

- Even when your child starts showing all the signs of readiness and success, please do not throw away your stock of unused diapers as they may need to use the diaper occasionally. Let's be realistic not idealistic.
- Keep drumming the benefits of using the potty into your child's head, instead of solely relying on the use of diapers.
- You can also use encouraging words and sentences such as, "Wearing underwear can be fun, do you want to try it?" or "If you use the potty, you will be able to learn to flush just like mom and dad."

- Do not be harsh or criticize your child if they still want to use a diaper sometimes.
- Do not remind them of their old baby habits—this may illicit a negative response in your child.
- A simple tip to remember in order to achieve a positive result from your potty training is to have your child wear loose pants which can be pulled up and down easily. Then, make your child repeatedly practice this step so that they can effortlessly pull down their pants and pull them back up before changing the diaper.
- Try to reduce the period between diaper changes and potty time.
- When possible, you should change your child's diaper in the same room where their potty seat is kept, as this strongly bolsters the link between the two.
- After your child has pooped in the diaper, they should be taken to the bathroom so that they can see you flush the potty. If you feel that your child is frightened by the flushing sound, this can be done later.
- Choose a potty that is long lasting and will not tip over if your child gets up to check their progress. Try to shop for the potty with your child and wrap it up as a gift for them.

- Some children may prefer the use of a potty seat (that sits on your adult toilet) as a grown-up option. When buying the potty seat, make sure it fits perfectly on your toilet so that it is not. A built in footrest is also a preferable option as it may also help your child to push during their bowel movement.

KEEP IT GOING

Potty training is a big achievement for parents, but for some it can be a bumpy ride. Take pleasure in the fact that you have laid the foundation and are making big gains. Below are some guidelines on how to keep your child's potty training moving forward:

- Start using pull ups so that your child can pull them down like underpants, but in the event of a mishap, these also have absorbent qualities like diapers. They can be easily ripped off instead of having to pull them over your child's feet. Once your child has achieved a few successes, you can try switching to washable cotton training pants.
- Keep them inspired by reminding them that using the potty means they are growing up. In the beginning, a small but appreciable

temptation can also be helpful as well. This incentive can be in many forms like putting a sticker on the reward chart or a penny in the piggy bank. As you child becomes more complacent using the potty, do away with the rewards and let your child's own motivation take over.

- Teach your child to check whether they are dry or not themselves. This will give your child a better feeling of control. If your child is dry, give them an appreciable pat on the back or a big hug but don't blame them if their diaper is wet.
- Try to be calm as it may take several weeks for even the most eager kids to achieve the desired results. If your expectations are unreal, it could affect your child's self-confidence.
- Avoid nagging your child if they make a mistake as nagging them frequently will only aggravate the situation and make them more stubborn.
- At the same time, do not force them to sit or stay on the potty. In the end, it is always your child's final decision whether to use the potty or not.
- Don't refuse to give your child drinks. Most parents believe that by restricting liquids, your

child's chances of having an accident will reduce. However, this type of approach is impractical, unhealthy, and not result oriented. In fact, a better approach is to increase your child's intake of liquids and thus give them more opportunities to achieve the desired results.

- Try to avoid a bathroom battle. Bickering over going to the potty will only prolong the struggle.
- Try some apps. There are some fun apps that are helpful in helping children understand and get excited about potty training.
- Have a potty party. It is all up to you whether you want to go all out or celebrate in a small-scale manner. Since the chances are that your child isn't the only one potty training right now, it won't be bad idea to invite some friends over to celebrate (and maybe get some positive reinforcement when they find out that all their friends are using the toilet as well). Another option could be to just have lunch together and a low-key celebration with just the two of you. Let them announce it themselves to their friends and family (for those who would understand and get excited) that they are potty training.

- Make a special phone call to grandma, or a favorite aunt or uncle who will cheer them on.
- Set a silly timer. For the first few days of potty training, I achieved the best results when my children went to the bathroom at consistent times. I personally started with every 20-30 minutes.
- Start a sticker chart. Sticker charts are advisable as they are a great way to encourage your children. Initially you can start by giving stickers each time your child goes to the potty. Later, switch to giving stickers for each day they stay dry. After you have achieved a certain target, take your child out for a treat.

As we all know, potty training doesn't come easily or without disappointments, and we must not underestimate the process. It is all about patience, waiting for signs of readiness in your child, setting the stage, and going for it.

CONSISTENCY IS KEY

Remember my friends, patience is the key to this entire process, but so is consistency. It is a milestone in your child's life, and you need to acknowledge it accordingly.

Potty training marks a developmental achievement of toddlerhood.

You and your child are in this together. They need your love and support along the way because they are dependent on you. Moreover, this journey will also help you two create a bond, and it sets the tone for your future relationship.

Following are some tips for consistency:

- **Repetition:** When you do things consistently with your child, they will pick up lessons faster. Moreover, once familiarized with the act, they will start feeling comfortable.
- **Demonstration:** Physical demonstration is an amazing way to teach your child. The lesson becomes ingrained in your child's brain. Children love copying their parents and siblings, so use it to your advantage.
- **Expectation:** You will begin this journey with high expectations, and that is natural. All parents think their children are great and will excel at whatever they set out to do. But let's be realistic and manage our expectations. All children are not the same; they are unique. Know that on average it takes around 8 months to successfully potty train your child.

- **Celebration:** It is the small things that matter in life. A smile, an encouraging word, and an affirmative nod go a long way in your child's learning journey. Don't be stingy with those loving and affirmative actions and words.
- **Enjoyment:** Lastly, have fun. Don't make it a serious learning curve. Stay positive, laugh at the mistakes, and support your child.

POTTY TRAINING REWARDS FOR OUR LITTLE ONES

Following are rewards you can give to your child whenever they try and when they succeed:

1. love, praise, and attention
2. reward chart
3. treasure chest
4. hand stamps
5. block tower
6. bathroom bubbles
7. fun time jar
8. books
9. sweet treats
10. screen time
11. big kid underwear
12. report their success

13. choose a big kid transition seat

Remember that potty training is not an overnight success story—it takes patience to get to the other end successfully, and you need to handle the process gracefully.

5

NIGHT-TIME POTTY TRAINING

Did you even know night-time potty training existed before you became a father? It does. Potty training doesn't come to a halt once the sun sets; your child's body is working 24 hours of the day. Let's delve into the night-time process.

WHY DOES NIGHT-TIME POTTY TRAINING TAKE LONGER?

Around 15% of healthily functioning 5-year-old children do not have the ability to stay dry throughout the night (*Bed Wetting*, 2020) . Moreover, about 10% of 6-year-old children will still require overnight protection such as a diaper or a mattress pad. You see, for your child to stay dry through the course of the night, they need to have a big enough bladder to hold the urine, or their brain needs to be mature. And this doesn't happen overnight after successful daytime potty training; it takes months or even a year.

IS MY CHILD READY FOR NIGHT-TIME POTTY TRAINING?

How will you know when your child is ready to let go off diapers during the night? It depends on the developmental readiness of your child, and keep in mind that every child has a different timeline for developmental readiness. However, one of the biggest signs of readiness is that your child can both go to the bathroom throughout the day and stay dry for a few nights.

Moreover, your child needs to be able use the bathroom independently. If your child is in a crib, then they are not ready for night-time training, which is okay. You can keep them in diapers for a little while longer and begin training whenever you feel they are ready.

TIPS FOR NIGHT-TIME POTTY-TRAINING SUCCESS

Following are some tips which will help you succeed at nighttime training:

- Purchase disposable sheet protectors.
- Limit liquid intake an hour before bedtime.
- Make them use the potty a half-hour before bed and right before they get into bed.
- If they wake up during the night, tell them to use the bathroom.
- Keep the way to the bathroom lit up, so they feel safe walking to it.
- Take consistent daytime potty breaks.
- Stay positive for yourself and your child.
- Be patient.

WHEN SHOULD I BE CONCERNED?

If your child is struggling with nighttime bedwetting, until 6 years or older, please try to practice more compassion and patience towards them, even though it is frustrating for you. You see, you aren't the only one struggling for them to achieve success, they are too. Since they have started grade school, there is also a certain self-image they would like to create, especially in front of their peers, so be sensitive towards them during this process.

Yes, delayed night-time potty training is normal, but if your child is still unable to hold their bladder by seven-years-old, then do take your child for a medical checkup. It will most likely be a developmental delay, but it is best to rule out any medical issues.

WHAT CAN I DO IF MY CHILD IS STILL WETTING THE BED OVERNIGHT?

Well, there is not much you can do other than patiently encourage your child and wait it out. Do not punish or scold your child, which will not work at all. Negative reactions from you will worsen the entire process. Try the following suggestions:

- Use diapers at night.
- Use rubber sheets or waterproof sheets during the night.
- Offer perks and rewards.
- See how an overnight wakeup call works for them.
- Wake your child during the night and put them on the potty seat.
- Manage your expectations.
- Give the process time.
- Don't look for perfection.

Be patient with your little one. It's going to take a while, and you need to follow your child's pace. You should keep your child in diapers for the night and follow the tips described in the chapter for easier nighttime potty training.

POTTY TRAINING A CHILD WITH SPECIAL NEEDS

P otty Training is one of the most essential parts of childcare, and all parents and caretakers must take on the task at some point. Although parents complain that potty training is a long, tiresome, and difficult process, most families have an easy experience of it. Even children who are reluctant and resist potty training and tend to be difficult about it eventually come around it and learn the basics.

Potty training is not the easiest for children with special needs, development delays, or disabilities such as Downs syndrome, cerebral palsy, autism, and mental development delays. Children who have special needs may require extra work and time to get used to the concept.

As with neurotypical children, parents need to understand that potty training will only work once your children are mentally and/or psychologically ready for it. Parents can start the process at any age (sometimes as early as few months) however it won't work until your child is ready. It is important to be aware of your child's development level before starting the process. Potty training for children with special needs can be hard as their physical, emotional, or cognitive development can be delayed. However, there are ways to make the process easier.

TRAINING CONSIDERATIONS

A child needs to feel safe and comfortable in their environment when any new change is introduced to them. This is especially true for children with special needs. Parents should avoid potty training if they sense anything out of the ordinary going on, if there is a change in the family dynamic, or if it is a stressful time. Furthermore, parents need to be patient and should not push their children into the process of learning. Parents also need to show support and encouragement through the process.

Being uncomfortable in a dirty diaper is a key indicator of preparedness and an incentive to start toilet training. If your child is not disturbed by a soiled or wet diaper, you may need to change them into ordinary underwear or training pants during daytime training. For children who are bothered by soiled diapers, they can continue to wear diapers or pull-ups, as you will still know when they are not clean.

As the development of motor skills can be slightly delayed in some children, they may have problems in potty training. They might need assistance getting on top of a toilet or getting undressed. Therefore, you may need to get a special potty chair or other adaptions. Once you have a chosen a potty chair and gotten it home, to keep your child's interest, you can ask them to decorate it with pictures and drawings or stickers. You can have your child sit on the chair while watching the iPad or indulge in any other activity, so they are more used to sitting on the potty chair.

For children with special needs, an especially important aspect of potty training is repetition. This includes scheduled potty training and repeating all actions each time. As outlined in the book *Toilet Training without Tears* by Dr. Charles E. Schaefer, this, "assures that your child has frequent opportunities to use the toilet." Whenever you see your child showing signs of the need to poop or pee, you must take your child to the potty chair and help them understand what needs to be done. Following the steps every time they go to the toilet will become ingrained in your child's mind, and they will repeat the same themselves. The process can also be broken down into smaller steps and done in phases if your child gets bored easily, gets distracted, or is not ready to sit for too long. You need be patient and not insist if your child shows resistance.

TIPS TO MAKE POTTY TRAINING EASIER

- **Frequent Potty Breaks:** Children should be made to use the potty frequently. Even if a child says no when asked, they should be taken to the potty as they may need to go.
- **Track When They Go:** It can be very helpful for parents and caregivers to keep track of when your child wets or soils their diaper. Children are likely to go after their meals or snacks. Therefore, frequent visits at the time will give the best potty-training results.
- **Model and Narrate Toileting Habits:** Children learn the most from their environment and have a need to mimic the actions of those around them, especially the adults. Therefore, one of the best ways of potty training includes modelling and narration. This is where you allow your child to observe you use the toilet.

Parents will also need to explain to your child the process.

- **Know Accidents are a Part of the Process:** Children can have accidents where they might soil their diapers or underwear at various stages of their potty-training process. It is completely normal for children to regress at times. They may also refuse the use of a potty. The complete process can take plenty of time, and it is important to understand that your child might have accidents during that time. Having accidents or occasionally refusing to use the potty is completely normal and should not be considered resistance.

RESISTANCE

For many children early on in their potty-training process, resistance, especially if they are not emotionally ready, is common. This resistance should be treated by discontinuing potty training for a few days or few weeks and then restarting. In addition, your child may need a lot of praise. This reward system can include things like snacks, stickers, or a small toy.

If you feel your child has a habit of resisting any change or new learning, you can preemptively take extra time to mentally prepare them for the upcoming training process. If you feel that your child is ready but is still resistant, speak to your pediatrician, get their opinion, have them examine your child, and get their feedback. Moreover, it is vital that you prepare yourself emotionally as well since it will be a challenge. You need to remind yourself that children with special needs have a different timeline with potty training and they usually complete this process by 5 or 7-years-old. For some children with special needs, learning to use the toilet can be painful. Always reach out for help and support because it goes a long way.

SPECIFIC CONSIDERATIONS

The first stop for help is your child's pediatrician. However, for children with special needs, an occupational therapist may be needed if your child has motor skill delays. These cause potty training to be problematic and difficult between the ages of three and five. Therefore, parents should not delay seeking professional help.

Physical Challenges

Physical disabilities can pose a challenge when it comes to potty training your child with special needs. Before beginning, note how your child's disability will affect different stages of potty training and how you will overcome this. Physical disabilities can range from not being able to sense the need to urinate, inability to sit on a toilet or just needing extra physical support.

Visual Impairments

If your child has visual disabilities, they will face challenges in the process of potty training. First, they will not be able to observe any family member using the toilet; therefore, they will be unable to mimic this behavior. Even simple actions we take for granted such as where the toilet is situated in the bathroom, how you sit on a toilet, how you reach out for toilet paper, and so on are difficult for a visually impaired child to pick up. Your child will have to fall back on language and verbal cues to understand the process. I would suggest you wait until your child is at least 3 years old until you begin their potty-training process for them to fully comprehend the process.

When you think you and your child are ready for the learning process, start taking your child to the bathroom with you. Allow them to explore the bathroom and figure out where the toilet is. Please see to bathroom hygiene when you are doing this and make sure the bathroom is smelling nice so that your child wants to return. Take it one step at a time:

1. Put your hands on their shoulder, so they can feel you sitting on the toilet.
2. Explain to them what you are doing and why you are doing it.
3. Hold their hand and guide it towards the toilet roll.
4. Hold their hand and show the garbage bin and how to flush.

This will familiarize your child with the bathroom. Once that is done, you can place their potty in the bathroom, take them to it, and allow them to get used to it. Remember to keep it situated in the same place throughout. When your child does start using the potty by themselves, please see that the passage to the bathroom is clear of any hindrances and that the bathroom is also an open space without any obstacles.

As your child familiarizes themselves with the bathroom and using it, make a point to visit bathrooms of places you visit frequently. Your child will better be able to understand the different layouts and styles of bathroom and will build more self-confidence. Make sure you reward all this progress with appreciation, praise, and hugs.

Hearing Disabilities

Children who have hearing disabilities may not find potty training too challenging; however, this will depend on their ability to communicate. If your child's sign language is good, you can convey to them what is expected. However, if your child is not well versed in sign language, wait until they are slightly older and then begin the process.

Remember to keep the training simple. As you begin to introduce the process, focus on the visual. Help your child observe you using the bathroom and show them pictorial books on it. Pick one gesture which denotes the following: pee, poop, wet, dry, and need to go. Use these gestures frequently so that your child begins to associate them with the action itself. Stay consistent and reward your child every time they succeed.

Continence Problems

Continence issues refer to your child not having any control over their bowel movements. This means that even if you have successfully potty trained your child, it can be difficult for your child to comply. And this can lead to your child getting frustrated—understandably so. I would suggest you put your child on a regular potty schedule. For instance, you can remind them to go to the bathroom every hour, which then will become a habit.

Cerebral Palsy

Children with cerebral palsy are slower in developing bladder control and do not have enough bladder awareness to start potty training by 2 or 3-years-old. You will need to assist and help your child develop their awareness of when they must use the bathroom. You can observe this through their actions such as holding their genitals or being fidgety.

Because your child will have limited physical movements, undeveloped muscles, and constipation (due to cerebral palsy medications), you must pay close attention to their diet. See that they eat enough fiber and drink a lot of water. When they begin practicing removing their clothes, make the process easier for them by adding Velcro fasteners to their clothes. You should also find a potty with sturdy side and back supports. For this I would recommend you get one that can be fixed into corners, since the position helps support your child. If your child requires further help, you can sit in a chair with a pot between your knees and have your child sit on your lap. With their back against you, hold them until they relieve themselves. With time, you can move toward a potty with sturdy and stable support.

Spina Bifida and Spinal Cord Injury

Children with these diagnoses rarely ever develop an awareness to use the bathroom, and few use the toilet properly.

However, you can help your child urinate through a catheter and you can help them visit the bathroom on a regular schedule. Make sure they are regularly eating meals that are high in fiber and liquids. Do note that sometimes your child may require an enema or stool softener. Moreover, make undressing easier for them by applying Velcro fasteners on their clothes.

Parents with children who have cerebral palsy and spina bifida can easily be overwhelmed and caught up with the need for special equipment that they overlook the cognitive and emotional part of this entire process.

When you do install the special potty in the bathroom, have a conversation with your child about bathroom usage and why it is vital to our healthy functioning. Let them observe you using the bathroom and reward them for the smallest of successful steps. There will be moments when your child will resist, but remain steadfast about the schedule you have made, unless your child becomes extremely resistant. Give your child all the knowledge, information, attention, and help when it comes to this matter.

It could be the smallest nudge towards building self-confidence.

Behavioral or Developmental Disorders

When it comes to behavioral disorders, knowledge of your child's strengths, weaknesses, interests, and tendencies will assist you through the process. Potty training children with diagnoses such as autism, fetal alcohol syndrome, oppositional defiant disorder, and attention deficit/hyperactivity disorder can be challenging.

Children in these categories may not be as motivated by or responsive to the typical aids such as, "wow what a big boy," or, "wow you can go potty on your own." However, small rewards are helpful. You will note that your child may find it difficult to adjust to new changes. They may be sensitive to touch or certain triggers. Children may become agitated over frequent dressing and undressing, unfamiliar spaces (such as the bathroom), and physical proximity with an adult. Moreover, children with may not mimic your behaviors which makes the process challenging as well. Hence, you may notice your child getting frustrated, angry, being stubborn and not cooperating.

Nearly all children with behavioral or developmental disorders can be potty trained, but keep in the mind that the process can take time. What you have to do is gauge whether your child is ready or not. You see, you cannot push your child. Do have your child assessed by their pediatrician as well.

While some parents start the training process with actual potty use (placing their child on the potty at an opportune moment and rewarding them for using it), others focus on the initial steps first. What are the initial steps? You can reward your child for even entering the bathroom, going towards the toilet, sitting on it, and then finally using it. Applaud each baby step because it matters. You can further make the process easier for your child and yourself by avoiding close physical proximity which may frustrate your child and stick to making your child wear only underwear.

Please note that your child may be resistant to learning this habit, so you will have to insist firmly, not harshly that they try their best. If accidents occur, which they will, you can show disapproval but do not criticize and punish your child. If your child grapples with verbal issues, keep instructions simple for them to comprehend. When your child does improve with time, it will get easier for you and for them. Remember, it is all about patience and hope. If you need support, ask for it; don't shy away from help. Accept that it is not an easy feat and remind yourself that you and your child will make it through.

Intellectual Disabilities

Children with intellectual disabilities can be potty trained, though it does take time. Remember not to compare your child's process with others. When your child can speak, manage their clothes, and display the awareness of needing to go, take it is a positive sign. Do keep in mind that simple is the way to go.

Keep the following tips in mind:

- Keep your explanations simple.
- Check their diaper every hour.
- Make signals which denote wet, dry, pee, poop, and need to go.
- Take them to the bathroom with you so they may observe you.
- Keep your actions simple for them to observe.
- If your child has siblings, have them observe how they use the bathroom.
- If they have a favorite toy, roleplay with it and display how the potty is used through the toy.
- When your child is ready, set them on the pot at regular times every day.
- Keep them on the potty for 5 to 10 minutes

while keeping them company (read, sing, play music and talk to them).
- Help them wipe themselves.
- Give them a reward. It can be anything from food, to a positive appreciation, to a hug.

As we end this chapter, I want to reiterate that you must take it one step at a time. Slow and steady is the order of the day. Your child is unique and will take their own time according to their personality, so do not compare and do not rush. Remember to keep your child motivated and determined rather than running towards the finishing line as soon as possible. Most importantly, be patient with yourself and take one step at a time.

7

POTTY TRAINING MULTIPLES

While I do not have twins, I do have a friend who does, and I asked him to help me write this chapter because I would rather give you firsthand knowledge.

You thought potty training your child was tough? Well, my friend, how does potty training two children at the same time sound? If you are parenting multiples, you need additional tips to get through the potty-training process seamlessly. It is twice the poop and twice the pee and twice the work!

HOW IS POTTY TRAINING MULTIPLES DIFFERENT?

To begin with, it is the number of children you are potty training. This could mean that you are potty training two toddlers at the same time, so you will have to have two of everything. Just make sure your twins have the same items, so they do not fight over anything.

COMMON QUESTIONS

There are some common questions that parents of twins will have. Well, I have all the answers to your questions so let's get going.

Q: What should I do if one twin is faster at potty training as opposed to the other?

A: Remember, when it comes to potty training, each child is unique and will process their journey according to their temperament and personality, so please respect that. However, keep in mind that if one twin gets it right, this can be a positive motivation for the other twin. Believe me when I say this helps the process. When one twin wants to pee, take the other twin along to the bathroom and encourage them to pee as well.

An important tip I would like to give is to set a timer for yourself. A timer that goes off every 20-30 minutes will serve as a reminder to put both twins on the toilet. This way you will have the twins doing potty training in tandem as opposed to running back and forth between the two of them.

Q: Do twins have to be potty trained at the exact same time?

A: Boy/girl twins usually learn potty training a year apart, but do not worry, that is natural.

Q: What if one twin is ready and the other is not?

A: That is completely okay. They will have different timelines, so don't stop potty training one twin just because the other is not ready. Moreover, don't push the twin who is not ready just because the other twin is. Respect their boundaries.

Q: How do you potty train twins if they are both of the same sex? Both girls? Or a boy and a girl?

A: It is a fact that boys take longer to potty train as opposed to girls. But know that personality types are a strong indicator of potty readiness. So, do not be deterred merely by the sex of your twins. There is a possibility that you can train them at the same time. If you are the parent of twin boys, you can show them how you use the bathroom, since they can observe and mimic your behavior. If you have twin girls, you can demonstrate with dolls to show the process.

Q: Is potty training twins double the trouble?

A: Simply put, no, it is not trouble, but it can be challenging. I know you can do it, so hang in there. It may seem challenging, but this too shall pass.

You will be anticipating and waiting for the day when your adorable twins will be potty trained and you can finally ditch the diapers, but it takes time, just like any process in life takes time, so be patient.

TIPS FOR TRAINING TWINS

▶ **Take time for potty preparation.**

At least a week before the potties arrive and are placed in the bathroom, begin a conversation around what is going to happen. Start potty training activities such as reading books on potty training and hyping the purchase of big girl or big boy underwear. Believe me, this is very exciting for children. Mia was overjoyed with her big girl Dora the Explorer underwear.

▶ **Get ready for bottomless business.**

As it is, the laundry load is high with toddlers, but then you multiply that by two, and suddenly, you've got yourself a laundromat. Spare yourself all that extra work (which I am sure you are doing singlehandedly since you are a single parent) and push your twins to potty train with bare bottoms at times. However, beware the random pee puddles you will find in the house.

▶ **Call in the reinforcements.**

Reach out for help; be it your babysitter, your mother, or your sibling. They can be of great help, especially while one twin is on the potty and the other is playing.

▶ **Employ a reward system.**

Applaud each success and be happily vocal about it. Even if it is the smallest feat, make it a big deal. Use sentences such as, "Oh wow, amazing!" and "Great, you did it!" whenever they poop or pee. Verbal praise is great, and so are action-based rewards, such as a hug, a dance, or a song. Your other children can even participate in this as well, even one who is not ready to use the toilet.

▶ **Do not use sticker charts.**

This should be a no-brainer. In the case of twins, a sticker chart will breed comparison, and that is the last thing you want. You don't want to put up a constant visual reminder of one's achievements.

▶ **Do not compare.**

You see, each of us are unique, and we all have our own way and timeline of learning things. Comparison is not always motivating, especially for twin toddlers, so refrain from giving examples. Focus on the individual successes and journeys.

▶ **Focus on good timing.**

Do not set a deadline for yourself or them. Remember, this is not a race. Take a look at the calendar and schedule potty training around time periods where you don't have to go for a vacation, before the start of preschool, or moving to a new place. There shouldn't be added pressure.

▶ **Invest in two potty seats.**

Purchase two potty seats because it is more convenient and easier for the twins. Even if your twins have their scheduled times, there will be an overlap, and it can lead to unnecessary fights. Purchase potty chairs and not inserts that are fitted into the toilet. Use spaces in the house, such as the playroom or living room for easy access for the twins.

▶ **Things will get messy.**

Accept the fact that there will be accidents and mistakes and prepare your home accordingly. Purchase cleaning supplies and protect areas of the house which you don't want to get messy. You can use baby gates to keep your twins out of areas you want to keep clean. Store the expensive carpets and sheets until they are potty trained. Remember my friend, stay patient and employ humor, it isn't army training—it is just potty training.

▶ **Flexibility is key.**

One method might work with one twin and another with the other twin, so be flexible. Tailor your responses individually for each twin. While one twin may respond well to praise, the other may respond to silent appreciation in the form of a smile or hug. You are their parent, so you will know better. Also, you may not always be with them so have a potty bag packed with cleaning supplies and puppy pads to protect car seats.

▶ **Have a consistent schedule.**

While potty training twins at the same time sounds wonderful, it may not always be that way. Try to keep them on the same schedule, without forcing or pushing either of them. For instance, I am sure you use the same eating, playing, and sleep schedules, so you can employ a potty time schedule as well. See how that works for you.

▶ **Dress for success.**

Who would have thought weather would be a factor in potty training? Well, it is. Did you know most parents choose to potty train when the weather is warmer because warm weather equals less clothes? Dress your twins in clothes that are easy to manage and easy to get out off. Consider Velcro, elastic waist pants, and skirts. Try to avoid buttons and zippers.

▶ **Mind your language.**

Try to create a positive environment. Offer positive reinforcements for when they do go to the bathroom and when they have accidents. Moreover, remember not to compare, I know I have said this quite a bit, but it is important. Do not use negative language, do not create a sense of shame, and do not use punitive measures. These are natural processes of the body, and your children need to feel comfortable with the process.

So, if you are a parent to twins, get going my friend!

A POTTY-TRAINING CHEAT SHEET

It's important to have the right equipment when preparing to toilet train your child.

This cheat sheet is your guide to making the toilet training process easier for you.

Please note that boys might require some additional gear. Additionally, I have included some potty-training travel gear essentials as well.

POTTY TRAINING PREP

A key transition for toddlers is moving from diapers to underwear. Potty training supplies may prove helpful to your child as they proceed through the different stages of toilet independence. Getting the basics is a good idea, even if you don't need everything at once.

The basic concepts are the same for girls and boys. It's about teaching them to control their bowels and bladder. Consequently, different equipment won't be needed for initial training. However, some things may be helpful as boy's transition from sitting to standing.

Toilet training boys is not necessarily harder. It really depends on the individual child and their readiness. Both girls and boys need lots of love and praise while learning this crucial skill. They both need encouragement and understanding about mistakes or messes that will occur. During this period, scolding or punishing will prolong training time or may cause regressions.

SEVEN MUST-HAVES FOR POTTY TRAINING

It's not necessary to have lots of gear for successful potty training, but you will need some items to assist the process. The decision for which products to choose comes down to personal preference, budget, and available space.

1. **Children's Potty Chairs:** These help them go to the bathroom more easily since they are miniature versions of the real thing. For

children to be able to sit down and stand up in a good chair, their feet must be flat on the floor while they are sitting down or standing up. Many options are available, but you and your child ultimately decide which one is best. You do have to clean them frequently and they take up space. Open-topped toilets and covered toilets are available.

2. **Toilet Seats:** These are also known as seat reducers. They can be adjusted and fitted into the regular toilet. A few come with steps to assist little children, which they can place their feet on while sitting. Seat reducers work well in small spaces. Moreover, you won't even have to clean or empty it out since all the waste can be flushed.

3. **Stepping Stool:** A step stool is useful for reaching the toilet and for washing hands after utilizing the potty. You can just purchase one and carry it around with you. The height depends on the usage. Decide whether you're using the stool for reaching the toilet or the sink.

4. **Underwear:** When your child starts to use the potty, sits on it, and urinates small amounts during the day, it is time to buy big kid underwear. Make this process fun and exciting

and take them along with you to pick what they like. Ask them to choose their favorite color, character, or texture. However, do see to the underwear being a loose and comfortable fit which will be easy to pull up and down. Also, keep in mind that when you begin to use underwear, accidents will be messier.

5. **Training Pants:** I would suggest you get cloth training pants only because they are convenient and great to use. Cloth training pants are made of light padding which is sewn into the center. This soaks up the smaller leaks and gives a wet sensation which helps your child. The best part: they're reusable. This makes them cost effective and environmentally friendly. However, if you want another option, you can also purchase disposable training pants. They will cost you more and you will have to replace them each time they get soiled. Do note that the texture of the disposable training pants is similar to diapers and may be confusing for your child if they are transitioning.

6. **Easily Removable Clothes:** When it comes to clothes, opt for the ones that you can pull up and down with ease. Clothes that are restrictive or obstructive will be annoying for you and your child and can lead to more accidents.

Avoid clothes with zips, laces, buttons, and rompers. Instead, opt for dresses, sweatpants, skirts, loose fitting shorts, and easy to wash cotton. When you are potty training, please don't buy expensive clothes. They will be stained by accidents. Keep it simple.
7. **Faucet Extender:** Toddlers are tiny; that is a given. Imagine your little one reaching for the sink to wash their hands. Impossible! Sometimes even step stools aren't enough for our little ones. So, what do we do? Invest in a faucet extender. It sounds technical, but it is very helpful. You can slip them onto your faucet and get them to the edge of the sink for your child to use. You can even buy the more colorful ones to make it more fun. Remember to keep the temperature of the water at 120º F so that your child does not burn their hands.

BOYS ONLY

Now we can get to potty training gear specifically for boys. At the end of the day, separate training gear is optional. You can see what you and your child are comfortable with.

- **Toilet Target:** If you choose to train your baby boy to pee while sitting, then you don't have to purchase this. However, if you are training your baby boy to stand and pee, then it will be useful for you. It helps him aim in the right direction rather than spraying all over the place. Toilet targets are available in fun and bright stickers, floating targets, and some boards.
- **Practice Urinal:** When you do head out to purchase a potty seat and chair, you can purchase this as well. They are smaller urinals and come in different shapes. You can either install them on your wall to make it like a real experience or get standalone ones. Some even come with flushes. While it is a very simple process, it is indeed a messy one, so do know what you are getting into before you train your baby boy to urinate this particular way.
- **Splash Guard:** If you are training your baby boy to sit and use the toilet, then a splash guard comes in handy to stop the spray. You can also get freestanding guards to use for your full-sized toilet, which can be used for older boys or children with special needs.

TRAVEL GEAR

Now, let's move on to potty training gear for travel purposes. You will want to keep the process going no matter where you are; be it on the road or heading for a vacation.

- **Foldable Seat Cover:** These rest on toilets and are like seat reducers. However, the difference is that you can fold this one and carry it with you wherever you go. I would suggest you buy the one with the washable carrying bag; it just makes life easier. You can fold it and put it into your diaper bag rather than lugging it around.
- **Travel Potty:** If you are on a long road trip and want to skip using the public bathroom, then purchase a travel potty. They are smaller and easier to carry around. One of the main differences between a travel potty and a potty seat at home is that the travel potty has a tight sealed handle and lid attached to it. This is convenient for when you want to empty the contents out later. Do make sure the lid always remains closed if you don't want a foul-smelling stench taking over your car ride.
- **Spare Clothes:** Always, and I repeat, always keep spare clothes with you. Keep them in the

diaper bag or leave them in a separate bag in the trunk of your car. There will always be accidents during the process of potty training, so it is better to be prepared. Keep an extra set of clothes, extra underwear, and wipes.

REMEMBER

If your child is resistant to potty training, you have tools to help motivate them! Every learning process does not have to be a boring lesson, it can also be fun. Here are time tools and tricks to make the process fun and entertaining for your resistant toddler. Some of these tools are also free!

- Tell your toddler they are doing a great job at potty training.
- Help them track their own progress chart and keep it reward based.
- Build their confidence by reassuring them.
- Buy bright progress charts with their favorite character to make it more interactive for them.
- Let them use activity books in the bathroom.
- Read them books in the bathroom.
- Rewards can come in the form of stickers, a hug, cookies, and so on.
- You can keep the bigger rewards for a big

milestone, such as going to the potty to poop on their own for the first time.
- Invest in bright and fragrant kid friendly soaps for them to use to wash their hands once they are done using the bathroom. It needs to be gentle on their skin.

Now that I have covered everything you will need for your child, let's get down to what you need to get for yourself and what you will need to do to get the process started. Yes, you are important in this process and must look after yourself as well.

- Purchase informative books.
- Watch YouTube videos.
- Decide which method you want to employ.
- Buy flushable wipes with which to clean the toilet. You won't need to be taking out the garbage thrice a day!
- Purchase cleaning supplies such as a toilet paper, wipes, soap, disinfectant spray, fragrant spray, mop, and a cleaning cloth. Keep a caddy with all these things in the bathroom within easy reach.
- Bedding is important to buy. Stock up on extra sheets, a waterproof mattress pad, and disposable mattress pads.

And there you have it. Now you know all the supplies needed to begin the process of potty training. Make a list of the things you don't have already and get them before you start potty training for a seamless experience.

9

TROUBLESHOOTING

When I was potty training my daughters, I found myself looking for solutions from Google and asking friends and family. I am sure you understand me. What are we supposed to do when we can't figure out why our little ones are regressing amongst other problems?

The potty-training process is filled with many dilemmas, and I bring you the answers in this chapter.

WHY WON'T MY CHILD POOP IN THE POTTY?

Many times parents exclaim they have had success with potty training because their child has learned to pee and there are barely any wet accidents, but the only issue is that they are not pooping on the potty. This is quite common, so do not fret. There are several things to take into consideration if you child is not pooping on the potty.

Fear

Usually, children who do not poop on the potty have a history of poop that hurt them. Poop pain is subjective. There is also painful constipation to consider. Even children who poop everyday can get constipated, which can be painful for some children. Make your child drink plenty of water, include a lot of fiber, and motivate them to be active to have a healthy functional bowel movement.

Even with proper diet, constipation can happen. Children who are busy and caught up with play and other things will only stop for a while, let a bit of poop out, and get back to what they were doing. Hence, the bowel is not completely empty, and the poop gets built up. When that happens, the body fails to give accurate cues for when they need to go. When they finally do poop, it can be painful. They might associate the pain with the potty. I went through such an experience with Mercy, and it was confusing for me at first. I read up on it and consulted the pediatrician who explained it to us. So, I feel your pain!

Do not lose hope, you can ensure your child that popping won't hurt. Though you will have to check for the consistency of their poop for weeks before you get them back on the potty. You can use stool softeners to further the cause. Moreover, talk to your child's doctor if you are concerned.

Position

Have you really thought about the process of pooping? Pooping successfully requires moving a mass of fecal matter through a tiny hole in our body. Muscles and nerves are involved in this process. Studies have shown there is an ideal position for optimal release, and it is called hip flexion—the knees must be slightly above the hips.

To aid the ideal position, you can invest in a small step stool. Make sure it is tall enough for them to place their feet flat on the surface and adjust their knees above their hips.

Process

Break the process into small steps which will be more doable and remember to praise their progress. In addition to small steps, make it a routine in your child's life. Repetition is key!

You can also employ the diaper as a tool. Have them stay in their underwear during the day and let them ask you for a diaper when they want to poop. Then, head to the bathroom, make your child wear the diaper, exit the bathroom while they poop, and make sure they remain in the bathroom to poop. When they are done, clean them up, put their underwear back on and praise them for asking for the diaper in a timely manner and doing a good job.

A few weeks later, make your child wear the diaper and make them sit on the potty while they poop. Repeat the process of cleaning and adorning big kid underwear again.

After this, cut a small hole in the diaper secretly. The next thing you know, your child is pooping in the potty. Make it known to them and say, "Look, you pooped while sitting on the potty. Wow, what a great job!" Over time, increase the size of the hole until they don't need the diaper support anymore.

HOW DO I AVOID POTTY POWER STRUGGLES?

Toddlers love the word no! This is the age where they are testing boundaries and trying to gain independence. Power struggles will be common, and when you add potty training to the mix, it seems overwhelming.

I know most of us ask, "Do you want to go potty?" because that is the polite way of doing it. But you will most probably get a negative response. Instead of asking, watch for cues such as:

- dancing around
- holding themselves
- freezing in place
- funny faces
- clenching their fists
- walking funny

Instead of asking them straight out, you could:

- Offer them a choice: "It seems you need to poop or pee, would you like to use the potty or the toilet?"
- Pose a challenge: "I bet you can't dance all the way to the potty." This will make it a fun challenge for them.
- When and then: Encourage them, if they ask you for a toy or for some extra screen time, then respond saying, "When you pee in potty then you can get your toy, etc."

Hopefully these tips can help you deal with any power struggle between you and your child.

HOW DO I GET MY CHILDCARE PROVIDER ON BOARD?

It is best to work together with your daycare provider since you cannot change the preschool or daycare's potty-training rules and policies. So, before you do send your child to a particular daycare or preschool make sure you ask about their potty-training policy and understand their policy on taking your child to the bathroom during school hours.

Every preschool and daycare will have different policies and rules, and this will also depend a lot on the ages of children enrolled there.

- Does the group consist of 2-year-olds?
- Is there a mix of children of 3 to 5-year-olds?
- Are the teachers in charge of taking your child to the bathroom every hour? Is there a fixed schedule?

Do communicate to your child what will happen at the daycare regarding potty training. Normalize the concept of using the potty while at preschool. Moreover, make sure you go to the daycare or preschool yourself and have a look around the bathroom for what the potty setup is like. This will help you understand the concept better and put you at ease as well. When you are touring the bathroom setup, ask:

- Where is the bathroom located and how far it is from the classroom?
- Which potty or toilet is being used? How high or low is the toilet? Can you send your potty chair?
- How high is the sink?
- Is there soap and a stepping stool for children?
- What is the privacy situation?

Moreover, also consider how the daycare or preschool handles accidents! It will vary from how you handle accidents at home, and that is okay. Know that you will not have control over every minute of activity in the daycare so have open communication with your child. Ask if there were accidents and what happened after. Through this you can gauge how they deal with accidents. Furthermore, send your child to daycare or preschool with the following reminders:

- Tell them where the bathroom is situated.
- Tell them it is okay to use the potty at daycare.
- Remind them that play time will still be available when you come back from the bathroom.

- Encourage them to ask a teacher for whatever help they need.

Do pack an extra bag for them to take to daycare. Pack some clean underwear, pants, socks, and a laundry bag. An important reminder I want to give you is that you should make your child wear manageable clothes without too many zips and buttons.

You need to be certain that the daycare you choose is the one you are most happy with in terms of cleanliness, system, vibe, and privacy. Also, you should know that most daycares and preschools are happy to work with you and take your issues into consideration.

Speak to your child's teacher about their potty-training progress and keep them in the loop. It makes everything much easier in terms of coordinating. Don't spring a surprise on them. If you plan on sending your child to school commando, please communicate that! Remember, they want to work with you, not against you. Be sure to communicate the following to your child's teacher:

- cues to look for when they need to go
- their patterns
- if they like to take a toy with them to the bathroom

Keep the following tips in mind when it comes to daycare and preschool:

- Ask for a clear-cut plan of action from the daycare and try to follow the same at home, since you want to be consistent and on the same page.
- Have clear lines of communication. Make sure you fill them in on how your potty-training process went over the weekend, if there were more accidents than usual, and so on.
- If your child is using a proper toilet at school, you can opt to not use the toddler toilet at home.
- Don't push your child if you think they are not ready. There will be numerous children who will already be potty trained at the daycare. Your child will get there too. Don't let the peer pressure get to you and go with the flow.
- Try not to use training diapers at home while using big kid underwear at school. Do not make it confusing for them, keep it simple and consistent.
- Trust the school administration to do their job but stay in the loop with them as well.

WHY IS MY CHILD REGRESSING?

Potty training regression takes place when your child starts having frequent accidents which could make your child go back to using diapers all over again. It is frustrating to the say the least, but you should know this is a normal and common phase of potty training. It can be fixed.

Causes

First, pinpoint the reason for regression. There are many possible causes.

- Your child was not potty trained properly: Proper and successful potty training is when your child sits on the potty and poops and pees. Ask yourself if that did, in fact, happen in the potty-training process.
- Stress levels could be high: Transitional times cause stress in children. For instance, if your child is starting preschool or daycare, they could be stressed. Therefore, regression could take place. I noticed this in Mia. She went through potty training regression when Mirabelle and I got divorced.
- Health issues: Constipation is a very common

issue in potty training regression. Get a regular checkup with their pediatrician and keep their diet rich with water and fiber.
- Easily distracted: Your child might not be able to sit with one task at hand for too long. They may not empty their bowel out properly because they are distracted by something else.
- The potty scares them: Some children are scared of the potty. They think a monster may come out, or they might fall in. The flushing sound may even give them a fright.
- Disappointment: Accidents and the feelings associated with them, such as guilt and shame, might also lead to potty training regression.

Solutions

Luckily, potty training regression is not long lasting; you can breathe now! It can take anywhere between a few days or weeks to help your child get back on track. If it is a medical issue, then I will strongly suggest you see a pediatrician. However, if potty training regression has anything to with distractions or changes, then the following steps may help you.

▶ **Do not punish your child for accidents.**

Do not show disappointment or shame them when an accident does occur. This will lead them to make negative associations and give them anxiety, which can lead to more problems. We do not want that, do we?

When you observe that your child is dry, smile, clap, or even praise them. However, if they are not dry, let them know that accidents are ok. Take them to try on the toilet anyway. This will normalize the process, and they will not feel shameful or guilty about it. Stay positive and empower your child. Please refrain from using harsh and scolding words.

▶ **Be gentle with your reminders.**

When accidents do occur, they usually happen because your child is having too much fun playing or partaking in an activity and doesn't want to stop. We adults do this as well, let's be honest. To rectify this situation, tell your child it is normal and okay to forget to use the potty at times. Assure them they are still a big kid and take them to the bathroom after, so you may clean them and change them.

Do ask their teachers to take them to the bathroom often as well. Do the same at home and give soft and gentle reminders from time to time to encourage your child to get back on track. Try to encourage them to use the bathroom when they wake up, before mealtimes, before bedtime, and when you are leaving home.

▶ **Employ a reward system.**

Offer your child motivations to stay dry. This will work well if the reward system worked for your child when you first potty trained them. For instance, give your child a cute and bright sticker every day they do not have an accident. Slowly, you can build this up to a bigger and more fun treat such as ice cream, a tiny toy, or a few extra minutes of play time. But be aware that rewards do not work with every child, and sometimes they may backfire. They might induce performance anxiety in your child.

▶ **Establish a proper schedule.**

Establish a simple potty schedule. The other option is that you remind your child to go after short intervals during the day. See what works best for you and your child. Make them sit on the potty for around 5 minutes after waking up and after meals. These times are when children will have active bowel movements. Remember to shower them with praise and attention for even making the smallest of efforts. After all, this is new territory, and a little motivation goes a long way.

▶ **Keep calm in the face of accidents.**

Accept that accidents will occur, and that is okay. You will have to clean them up but do it in a calm manner without scolding your child. Try not to be harsh and do not overreact to accidents. Try to stay clear from power struggles and do not reinforce negative behaviors.

Potty training regression is not a setback, it is a normal occurrence which can be treated, so do not fret!

TIME FOR ACTION!

Here we are, at the end of this journey. From the beginning to the end, I have tried to cover all the aspects that would be of importance to you. I feel your challenges, your pain, and your impatience because I too have been there. That is why I compiled everything for you over a period of years. The topics that have been covered throughout the book include:

- lessons from potty training
- perfect timing
- the methods
- nighttime potty training
- potty training a child with special needs
- potty training multiples
- troubleshooting and tips

I know how challenging it is, and it is very normal. Just remember:

- You may be ready, but your child may not be ready.
- They won't stay seated on the potty and may run around everywhere.
- Accidents are normal.
- Potty training regression is a part of the journey.
- Stay calm and cool even though it is easy to get frustrated. Remember your child will respond to your reactions.
- Each child is different, and you need to understand that.
- Preparation is key.
- Patience is key. Learn to stay patient with your little one through all the ups and downs of the potty-training journey.
- Learn to make your child responsible for their body.
- Make your child a part of the process.
- Make accidents a nonchalant process.
- Don't embarrass or shame your child, no matter what your expectations are from your child.
- Be consistent in your effort and methods.
- Be persistent.

- Manage your expectations.
- Laugh at the mistakes.
- It takes time; there is no hurry.

I hope you have learned enough about the process of potty training and can adapt it to your child. Pick which method you want to use, make use of all my tips and tricks, and learn from my mistakes. Remember this book is a step-by-step guide to potty training your toddler, so everything is covered.

Now that you are empowered with the information you need to kick start your potty-training journey successfully, let's get started. Good luck my friend, I have full faith you can do this!

Please consider recommending this book to your spouse and friends so that you can all be a great army of parents who are tackling potty training as it comes! Who turns down more support when it comes to taking care of children? (especially if you are a single father) I would appreciate it if you could leave a review on the book in the comments section. Thank you!

QUICK NOTE

Positive reviews from awesome customers like you help others to feel confident about choosing this book too. Could you take 60 seconds on Amazon or any platform where you got the book and share your happy experiences? There are other awesome books like *The First Time Father, The First Time Father: Baby's First Year, Sleep Training like a Pro, Single Dad Parenting like a Pro, Potty Training Like a Pro, Discipline Like a Pro, All Fathers Memorable Jokes* and others still to come. Any ideas you would like Alfie Thomas to write about or improve on, his email is always open. You can reach out to:

books@alfie-thomas.com

https://thealfiethomas.com/

https://mirabellen.activehosted.com/f/1

https://www.facebook.com/groups/1253933881690907

https://www.instagram.com/alfiethomas.official/

We will be forever grateful. Thank you in advance for helping us out.

BIBLIOGRAPHY

Average age for potty training boys and girls: Tips and more. (2018, July 23). Healthline. https://www.healthline.com/health/parenting/average-age-for-potty-training

Bed wetting: How you can help your child stay dry at night. (2020, March 12). Latrobe Community Health Service. https://www.lchs.com.au/news-and-media/bed-wetting-how-you-can-help-your-child-stay-dry-at-night/

Kiddoo, D. A. (2012). Toilet training children: When to start and how to train. *CMAJ : Canadian Medical Association Journal, 184*(5), 511. https://doi.org/10.1503/cmaj.110830

Potty train in 3 days: Is it possible? (2016, February 12). Healthline. https://www.healthline.com/health/parenting/potty-train-in-three-days

What toilet training teaches you. (n.d.). HealthyChildren.Org. https://www.healthychildren.org/English/ages-stages/toddler/toilet-training/Pages/What-Toilet-Training-Teaches-You.aspx

www.ingramcontent.com/pod-product-compliance
Lightning Source LLC
Chambersburg PA
CBHW040510110526
44587CB00045B/4194